Birds and Butterflies

Coloring Book

Original Hand Drawn Images for Relaxation

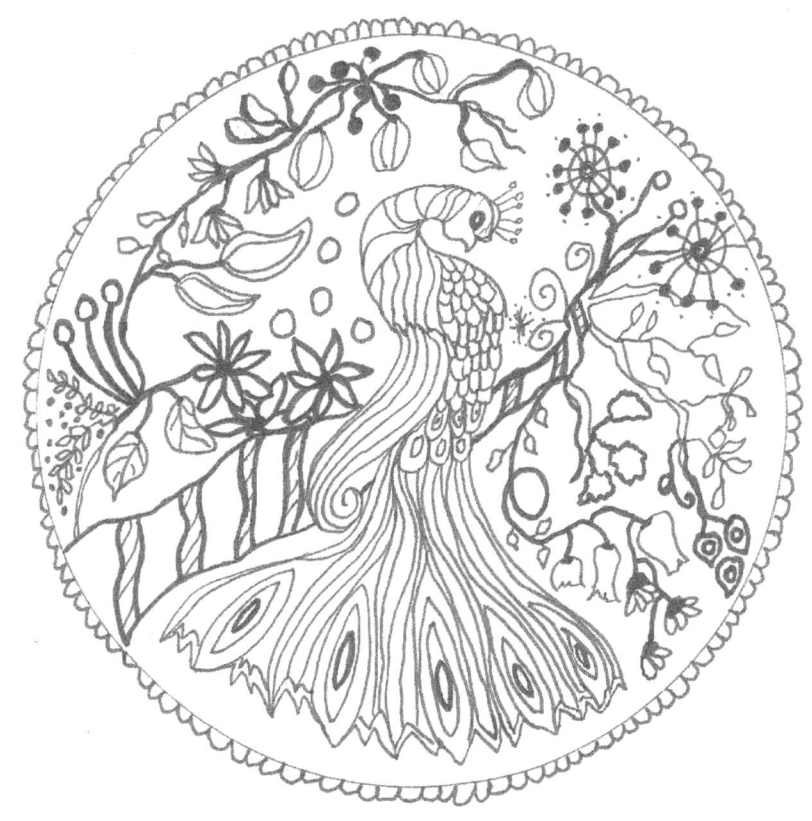

By: Kaye Dennan

KD Coloring Studio

http://kdcoloring.com

ISBN-13: 978-1533268860

Sample Graphics from this Book

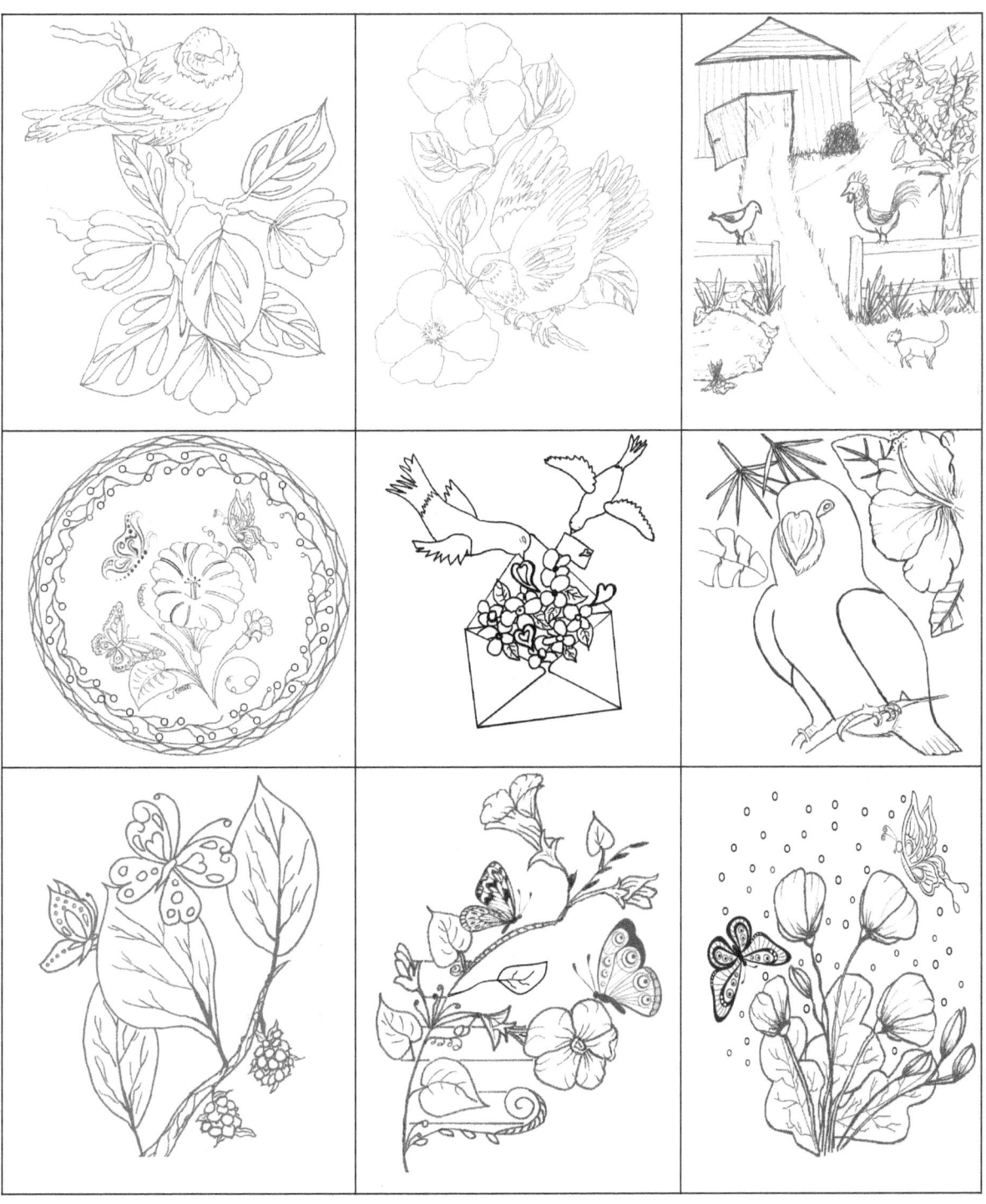

PUBLISHERS NOTES
Disclaimer

Paperback Edition

Manufactured in the United States of America

Kaye Dennan

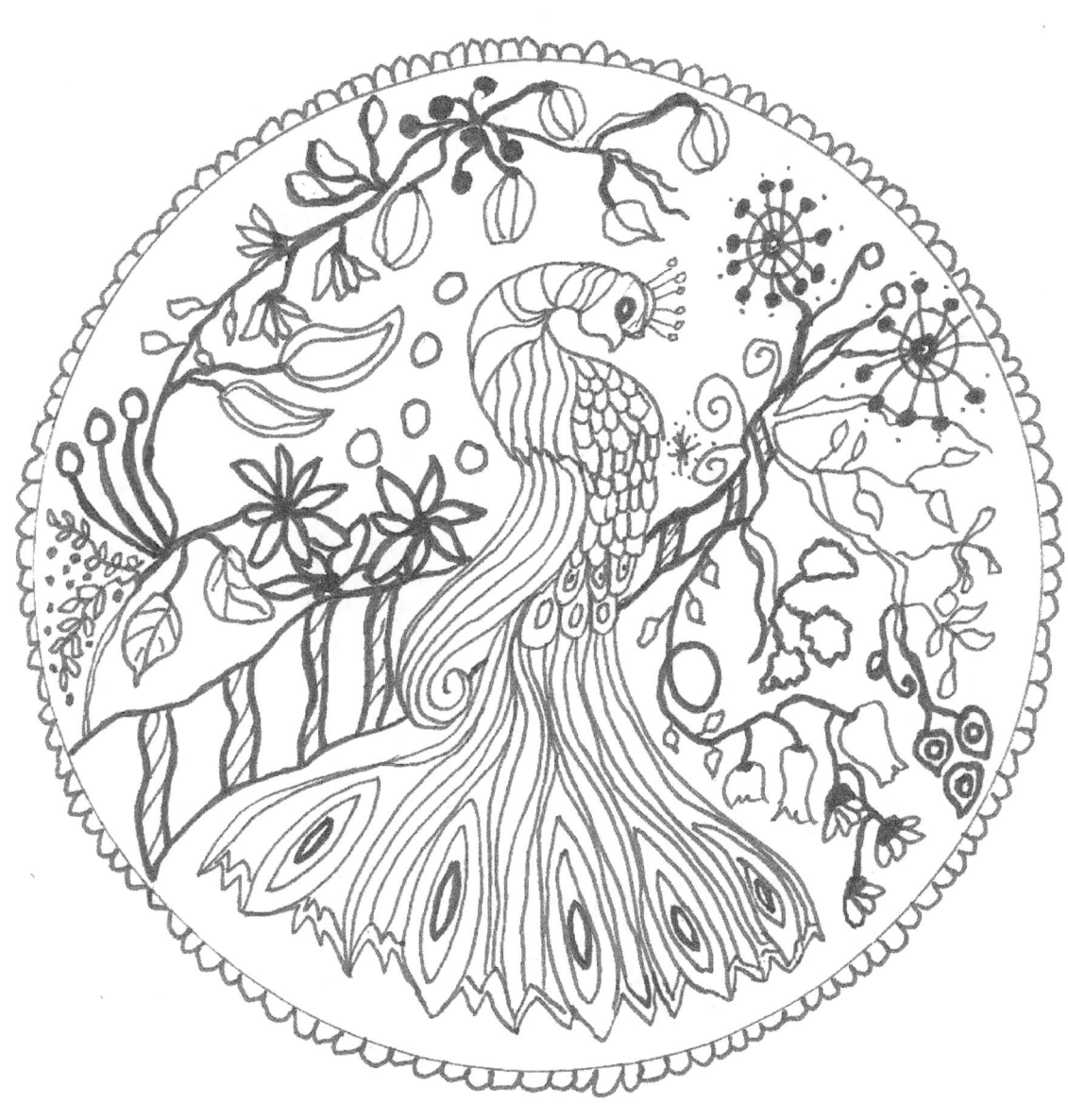

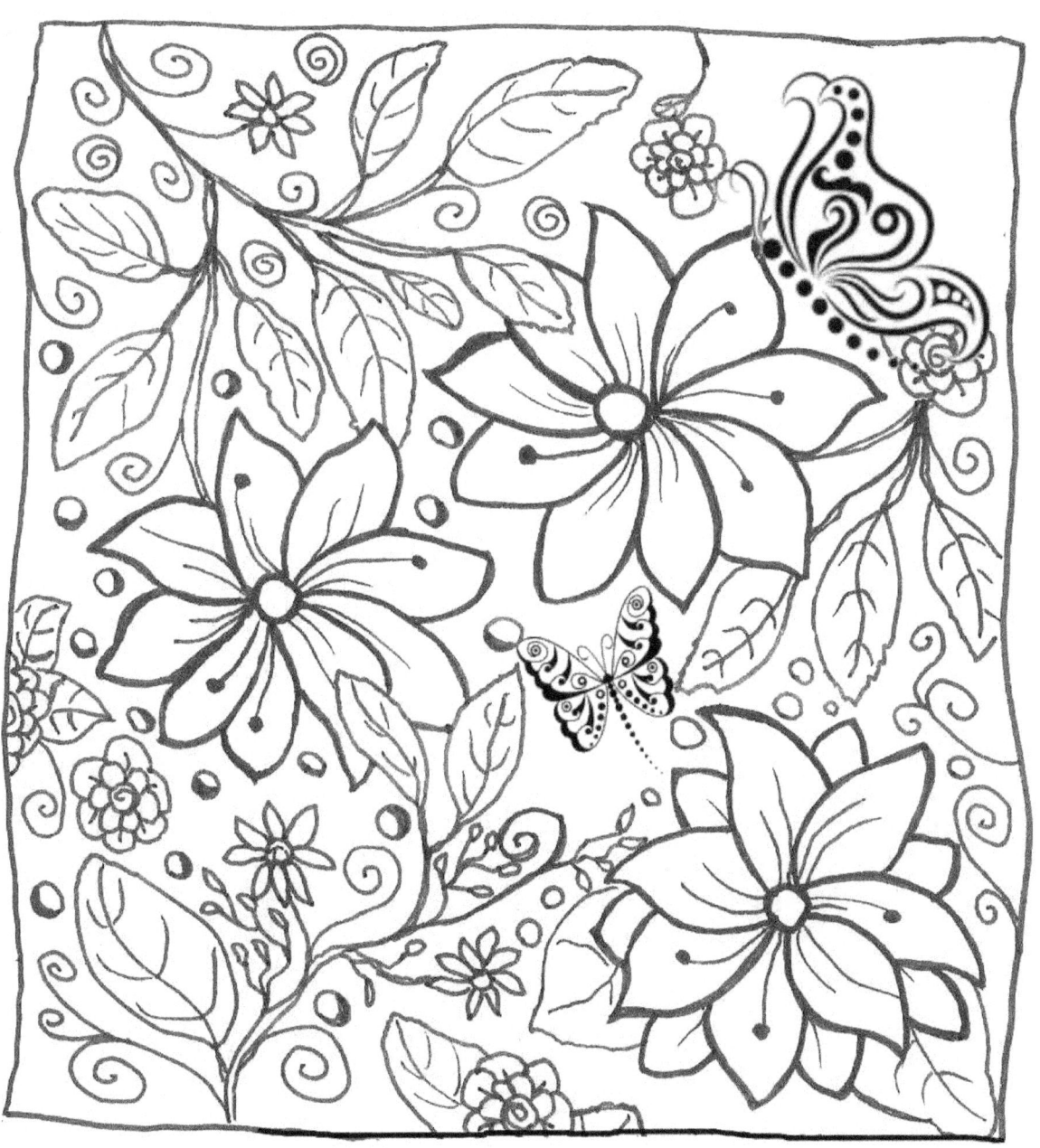

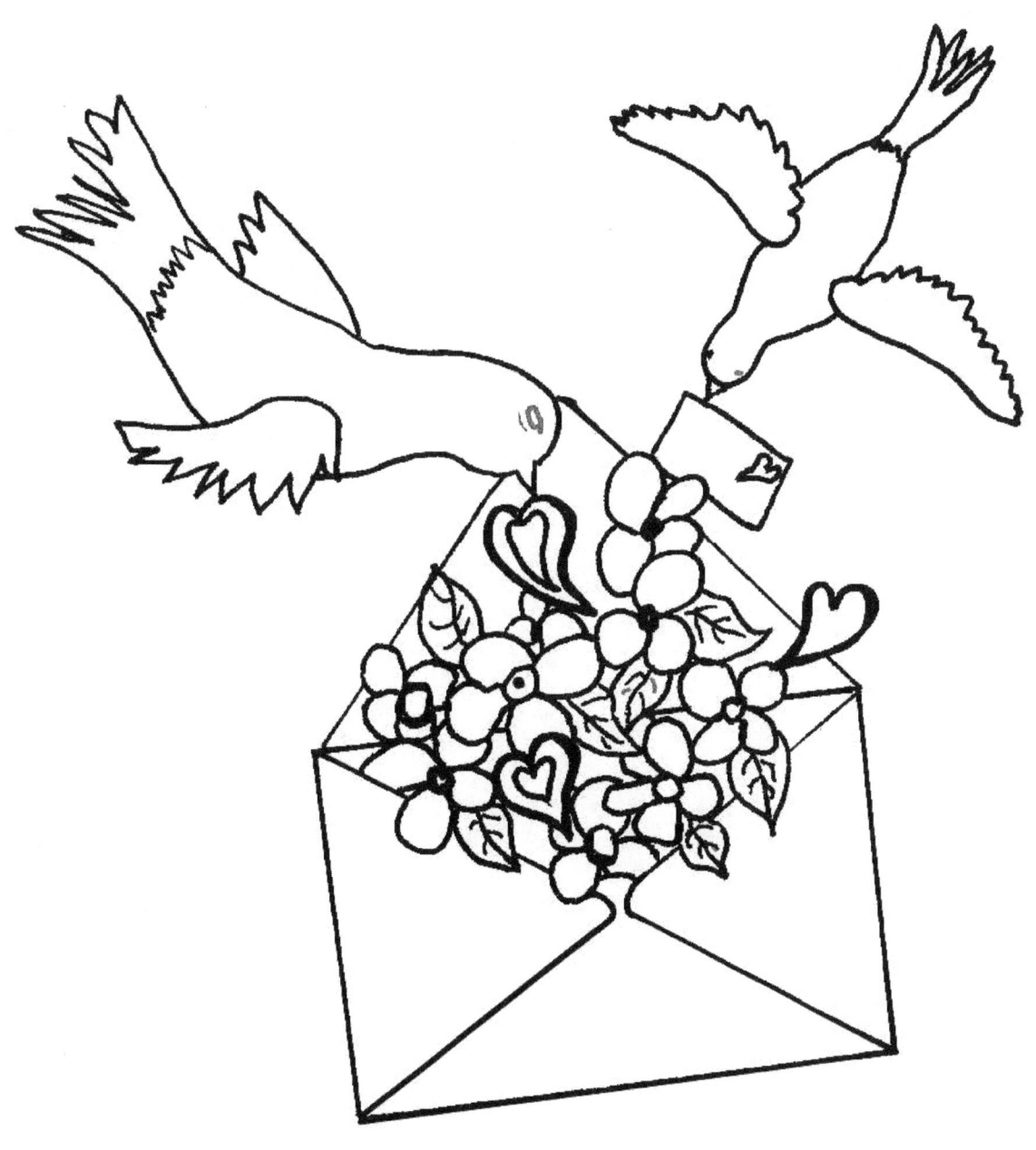

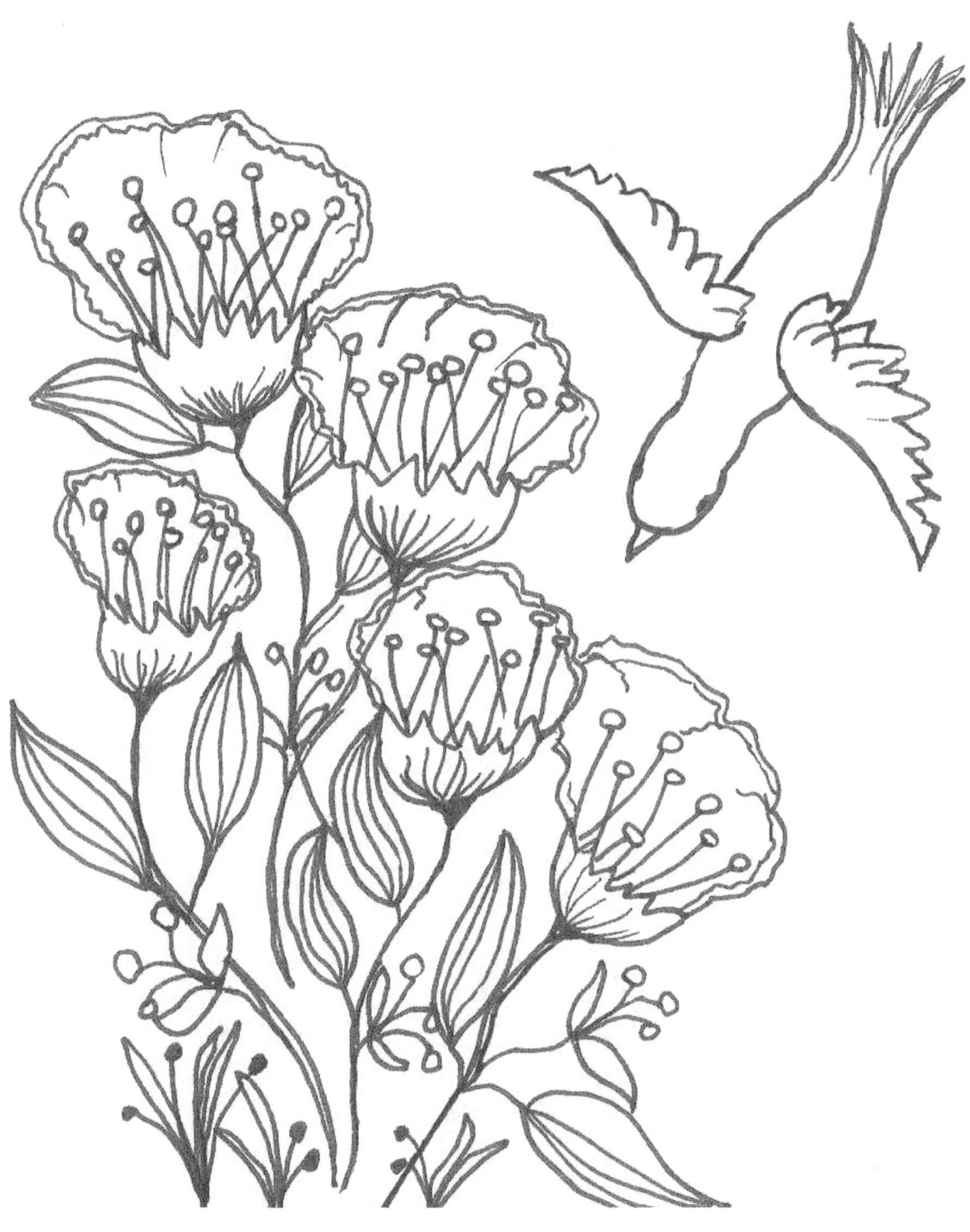

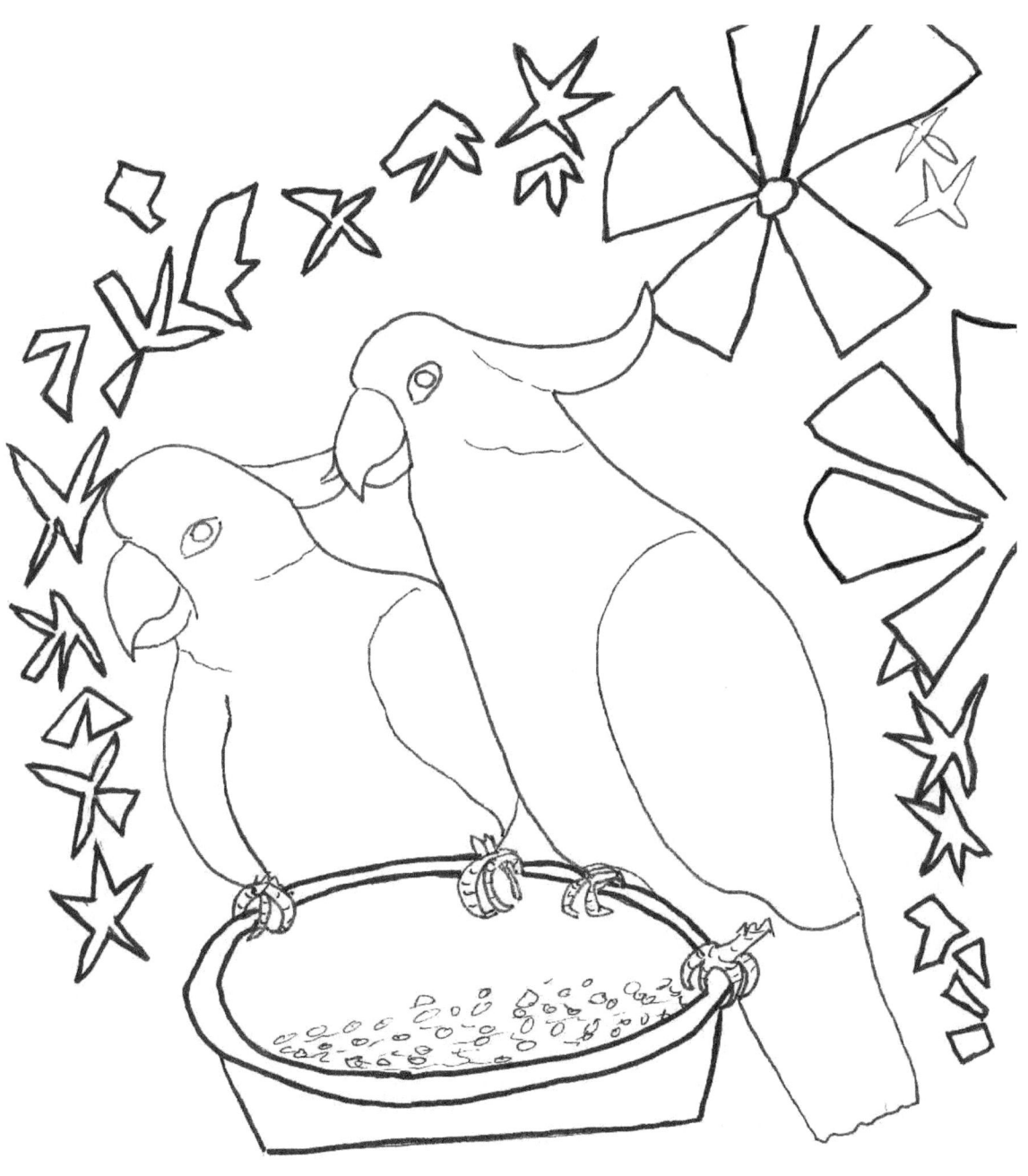

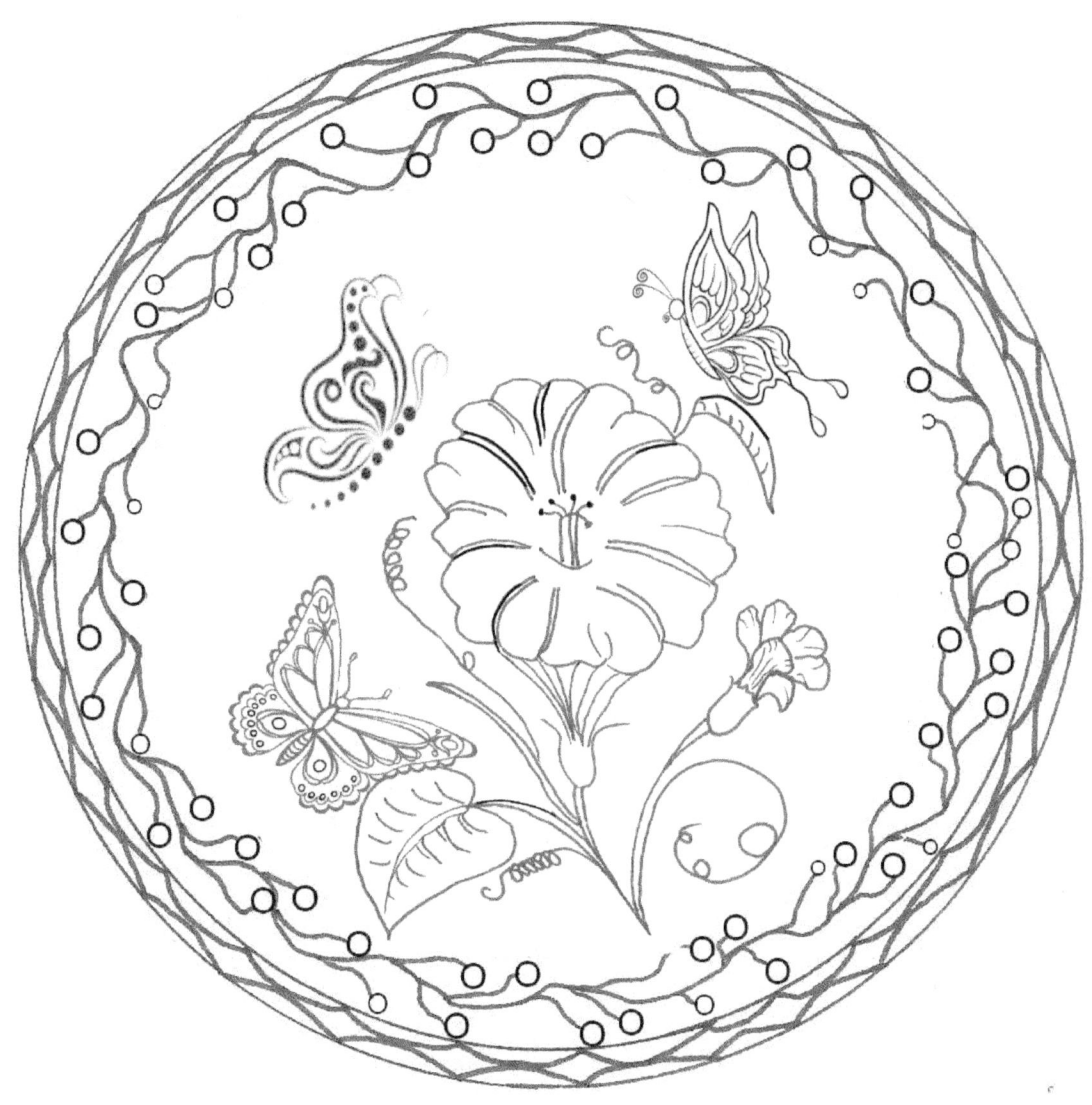

Kaye Dennan

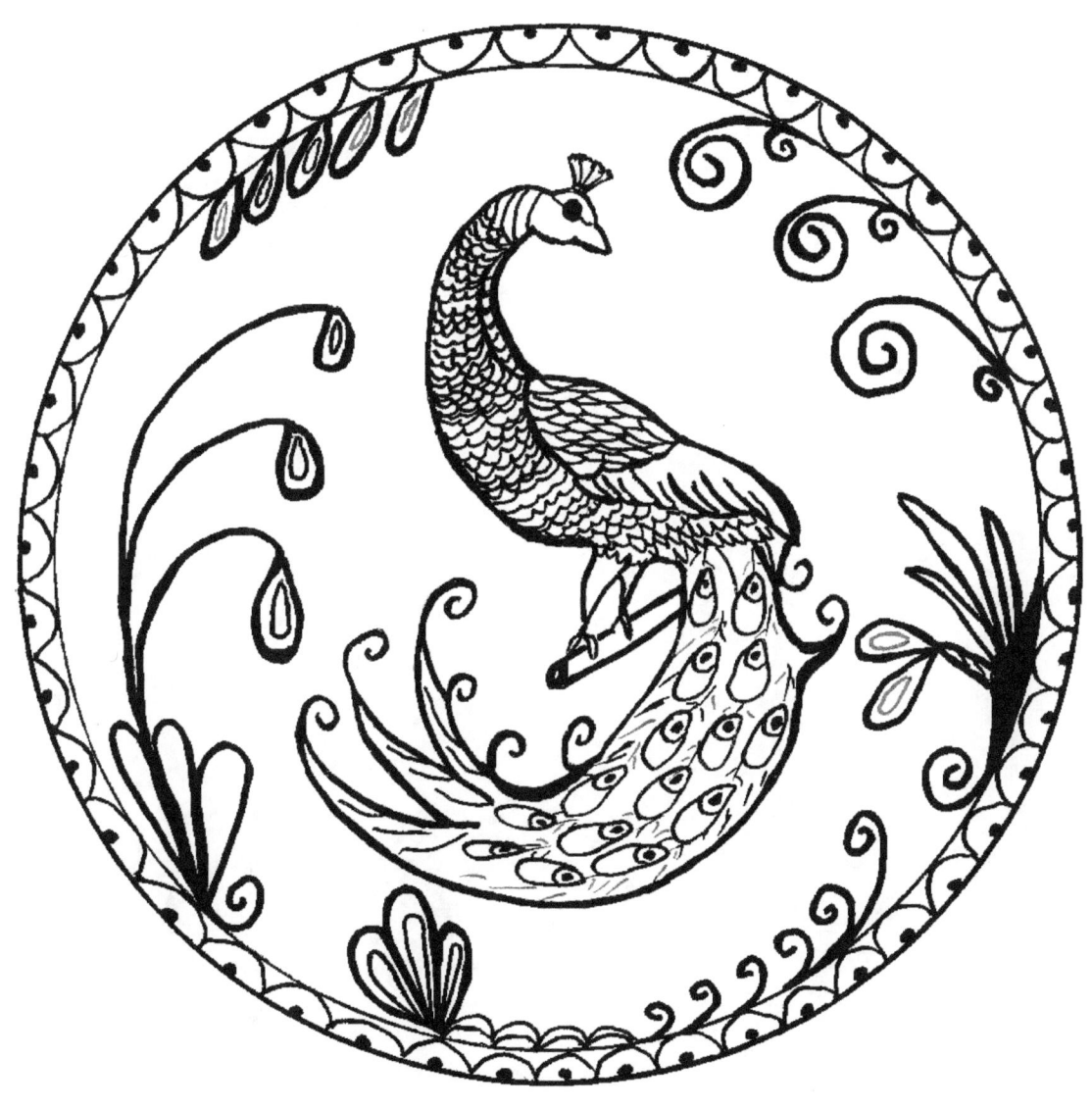

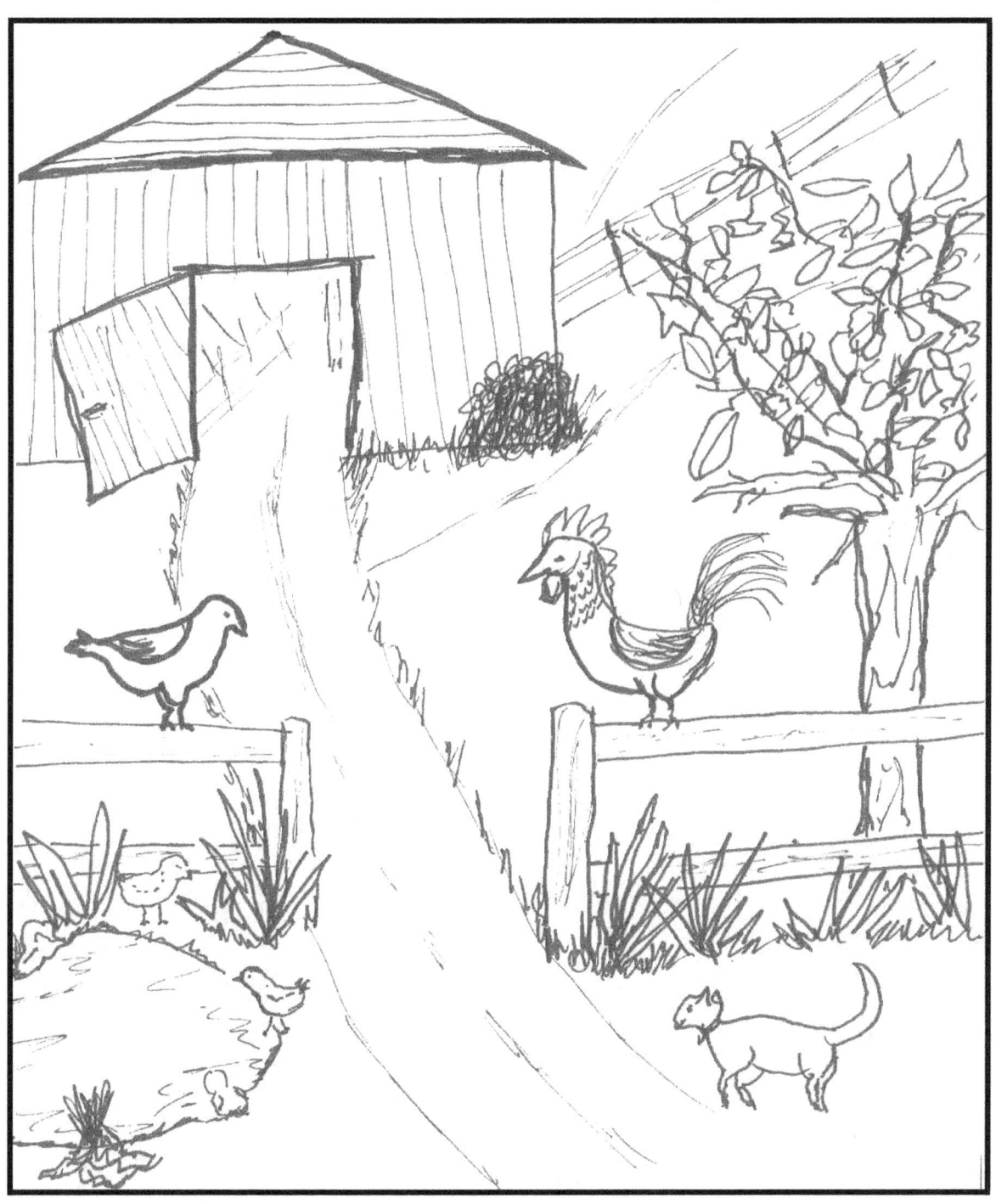

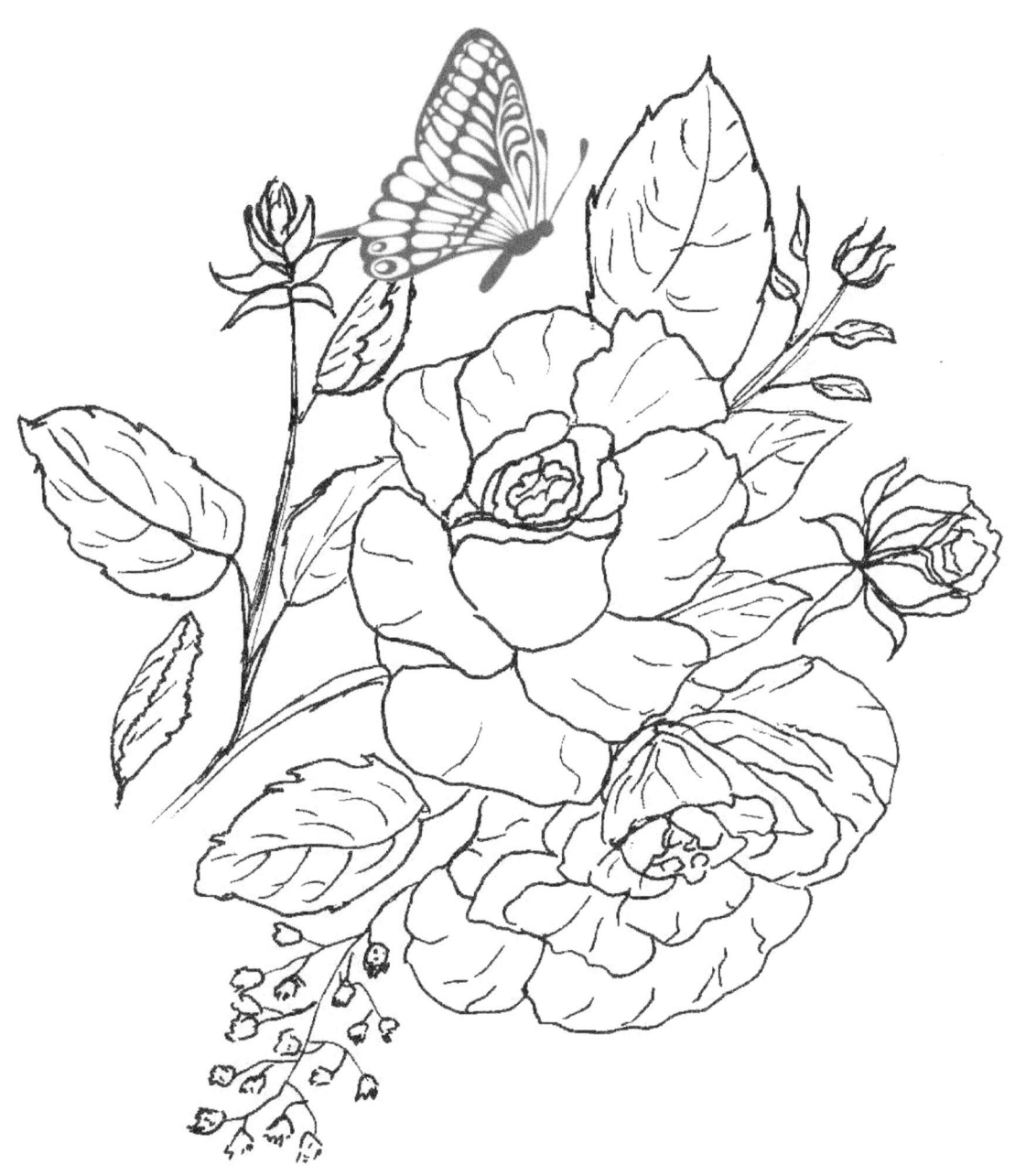

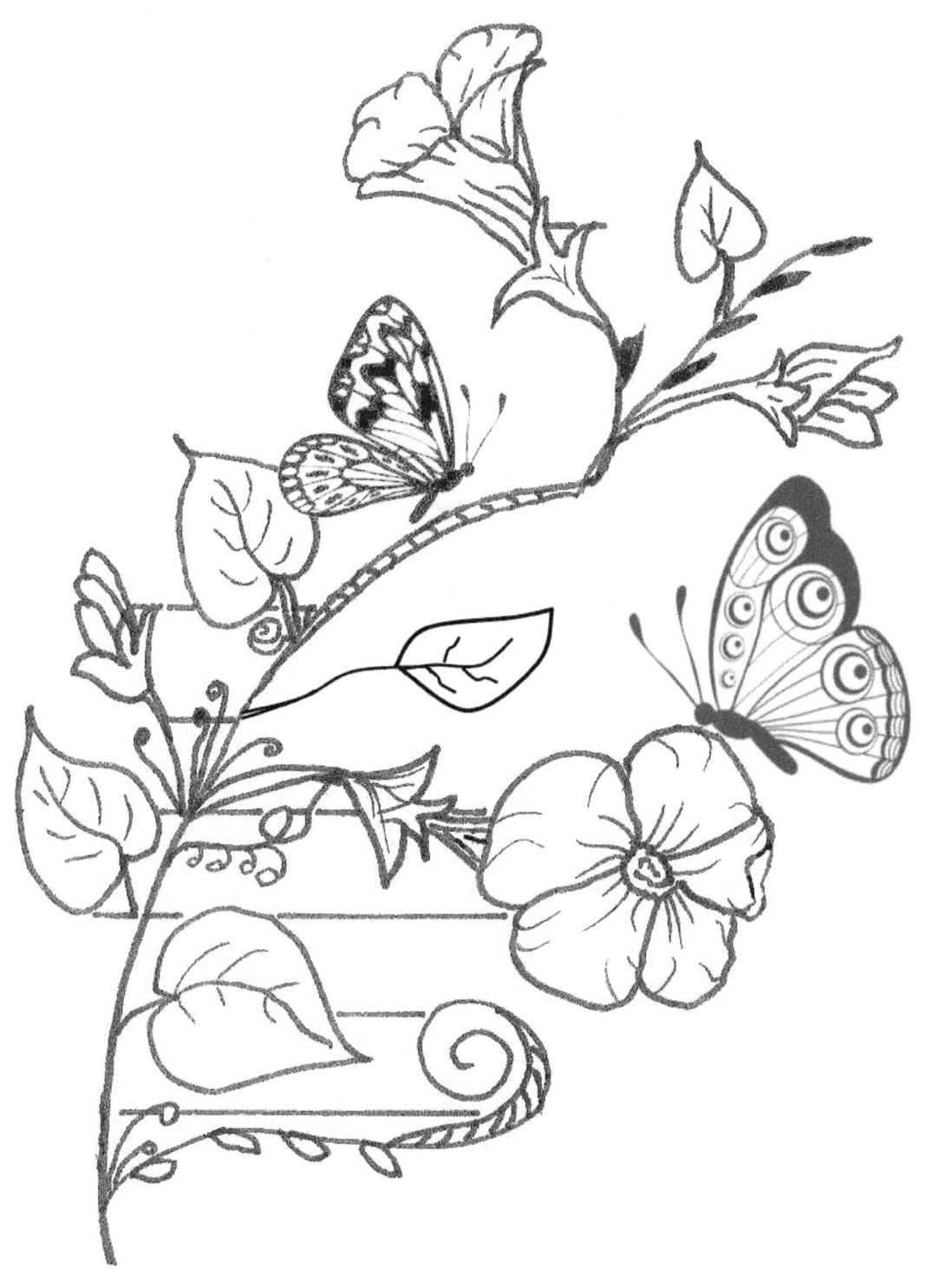

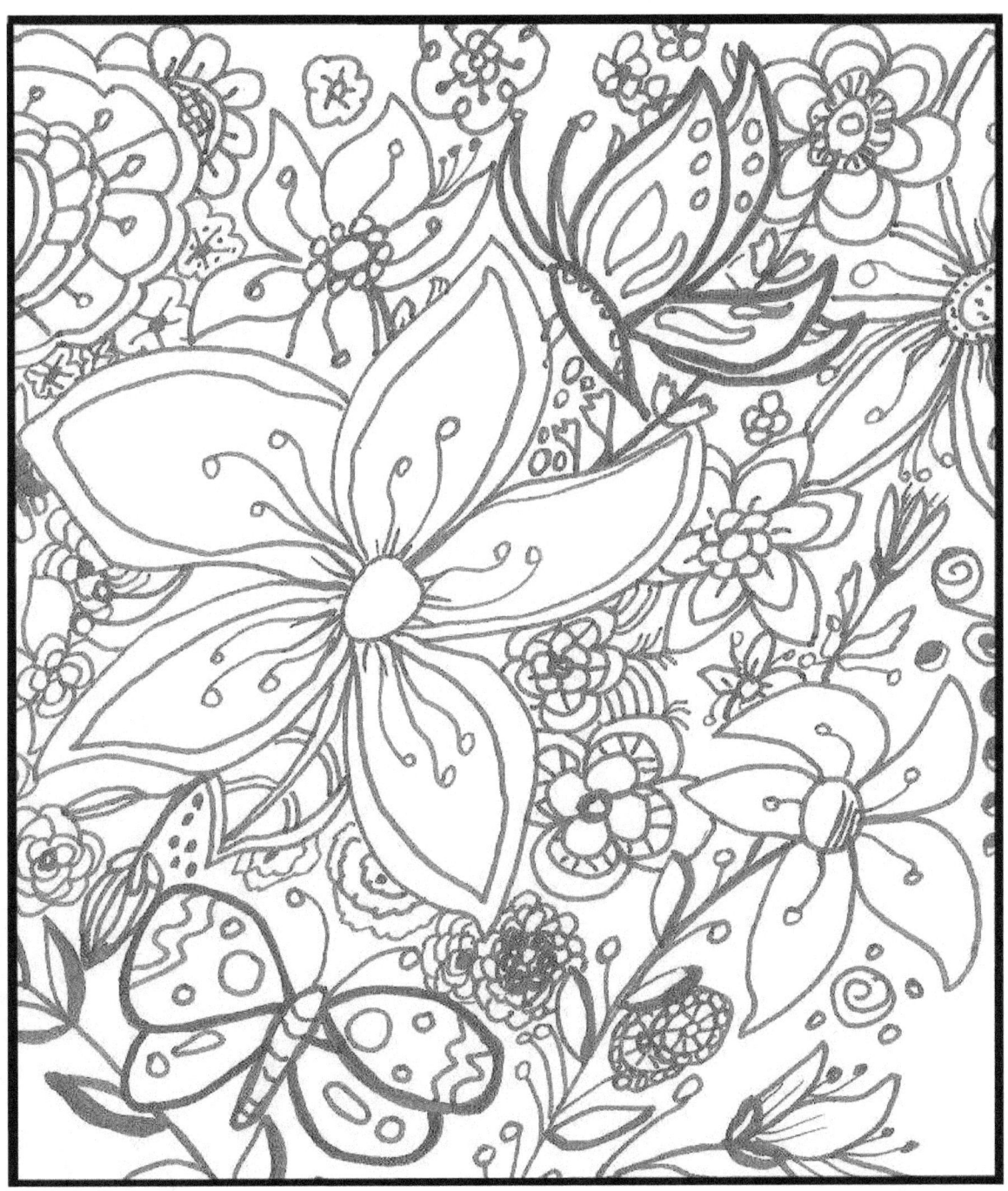

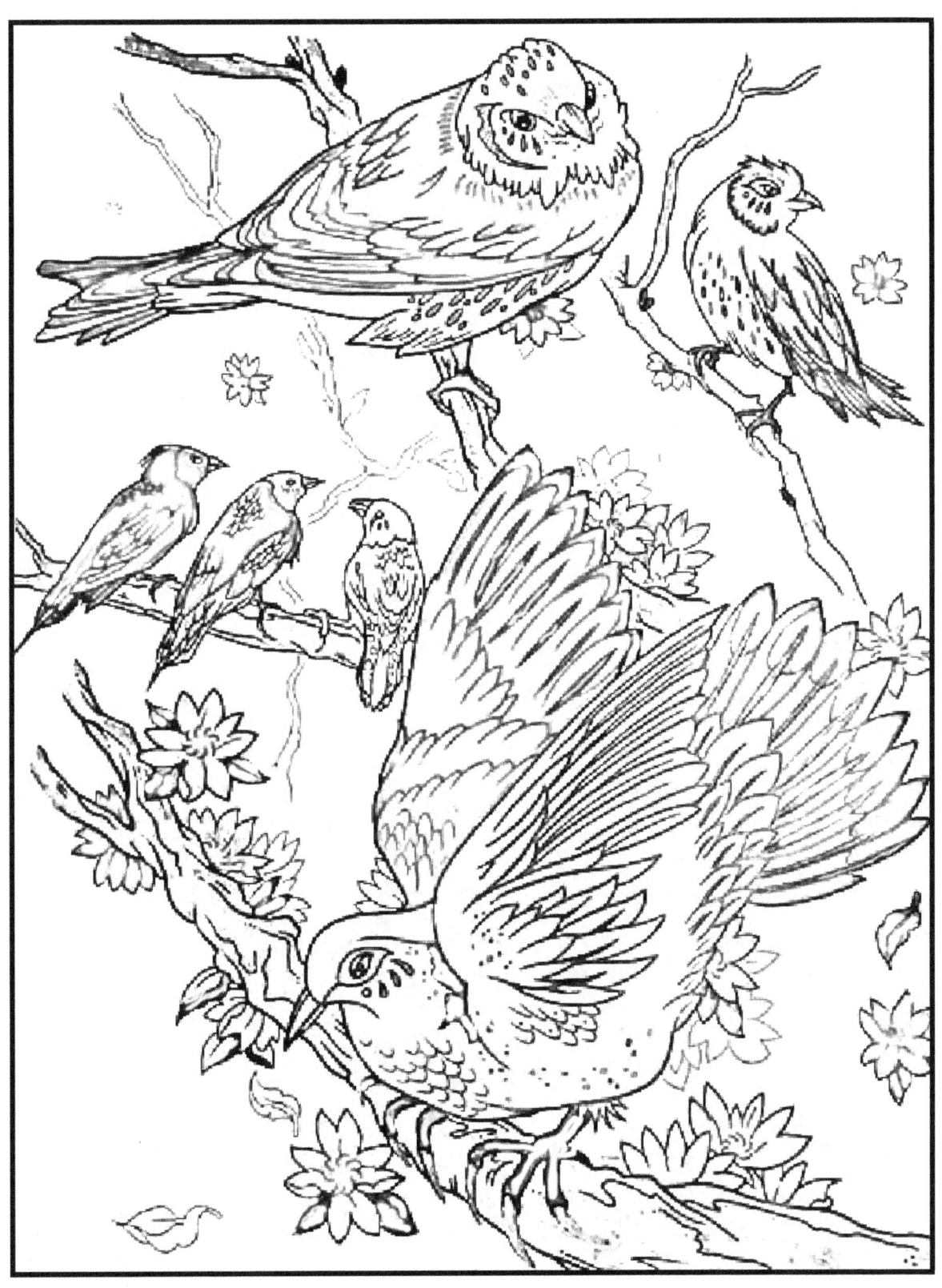

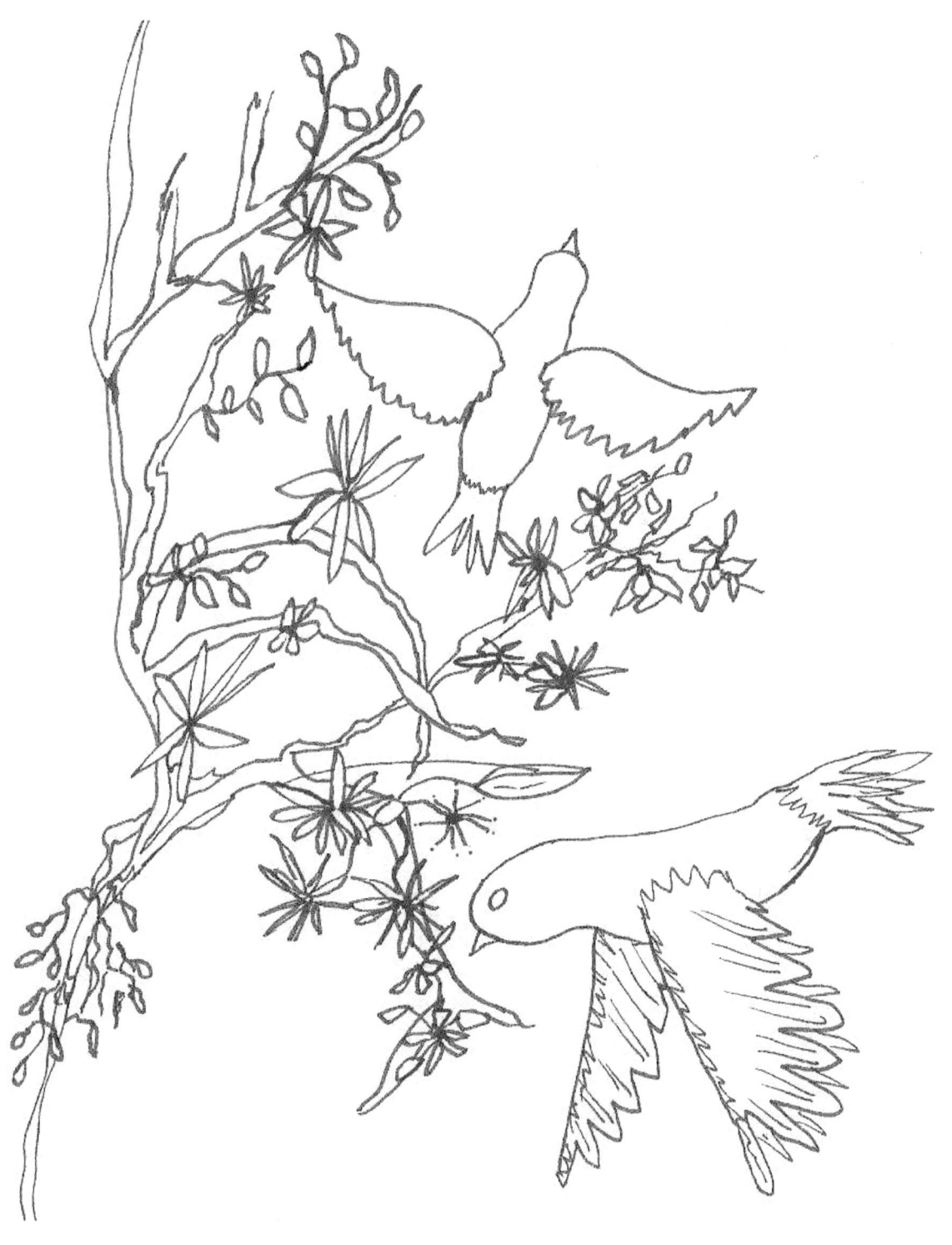

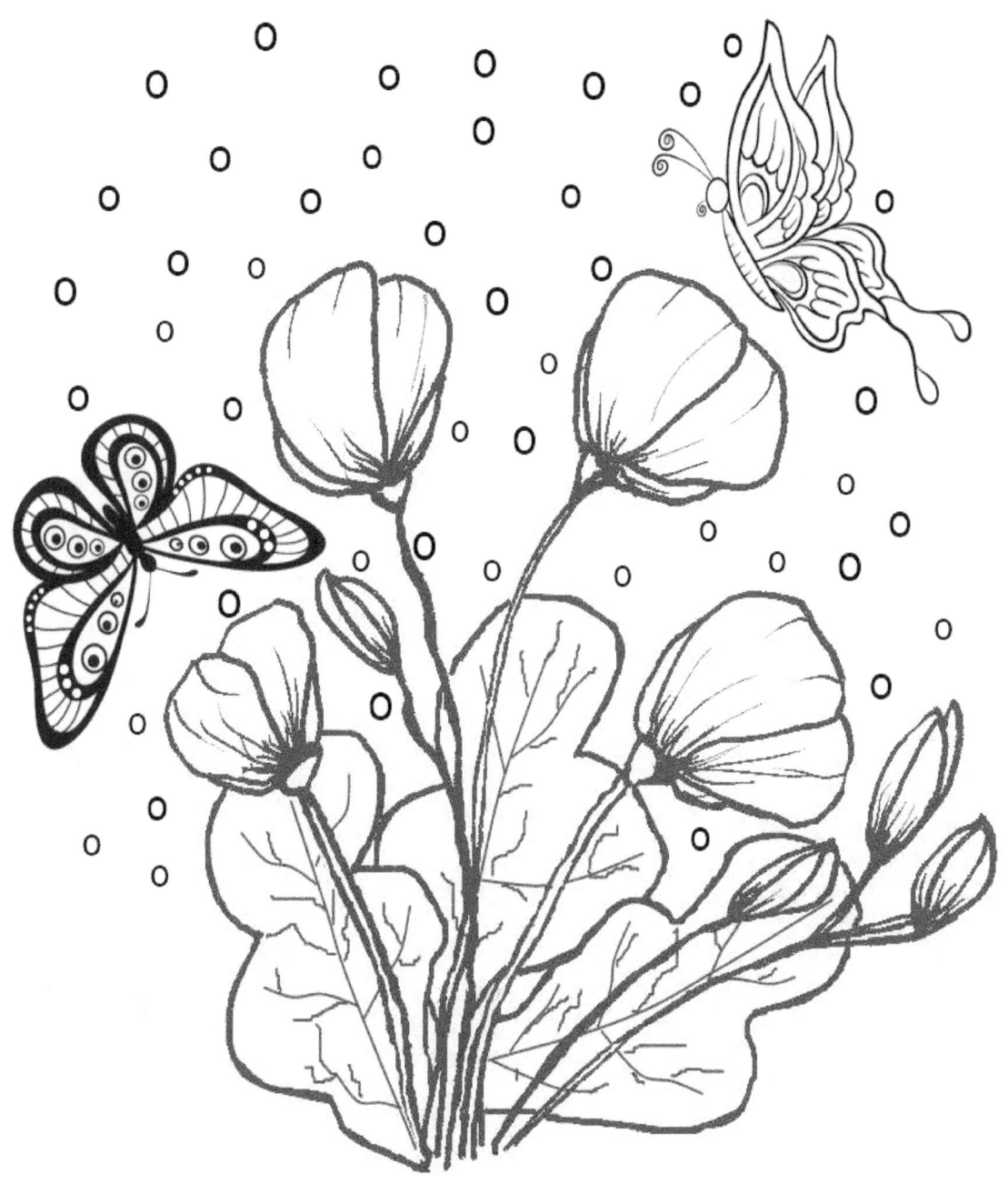

KD COLORING STUDIO

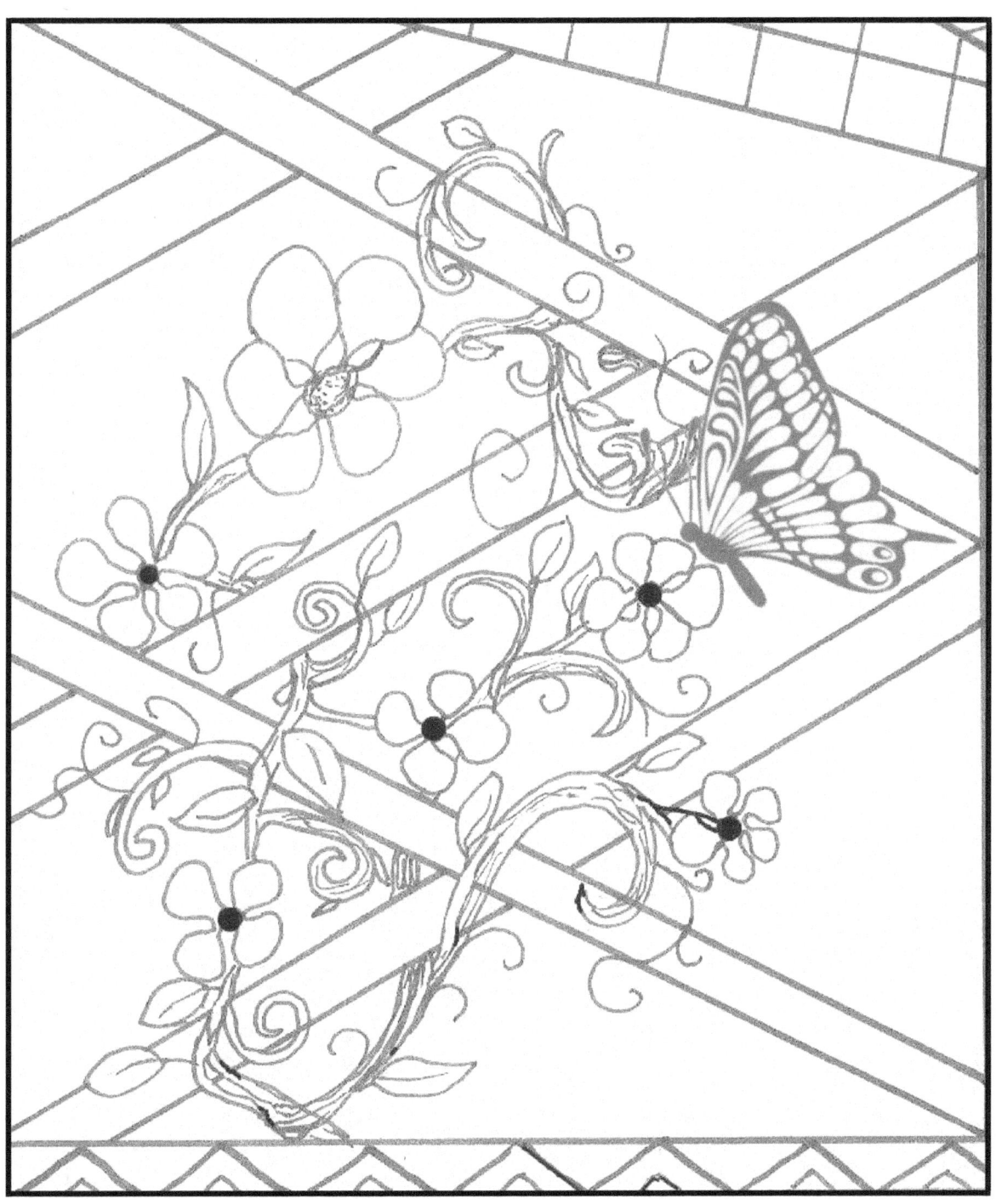

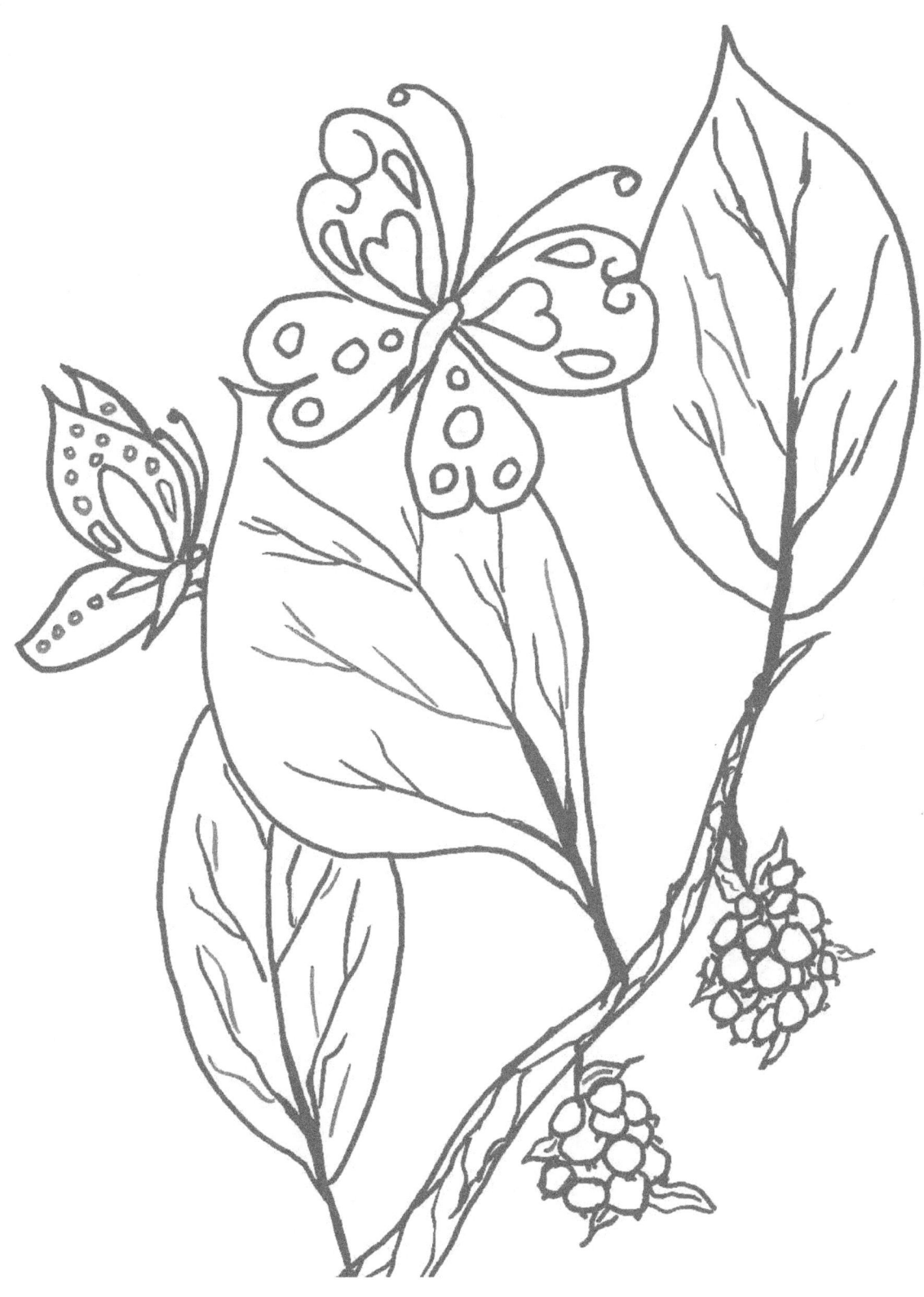

Honeyeater

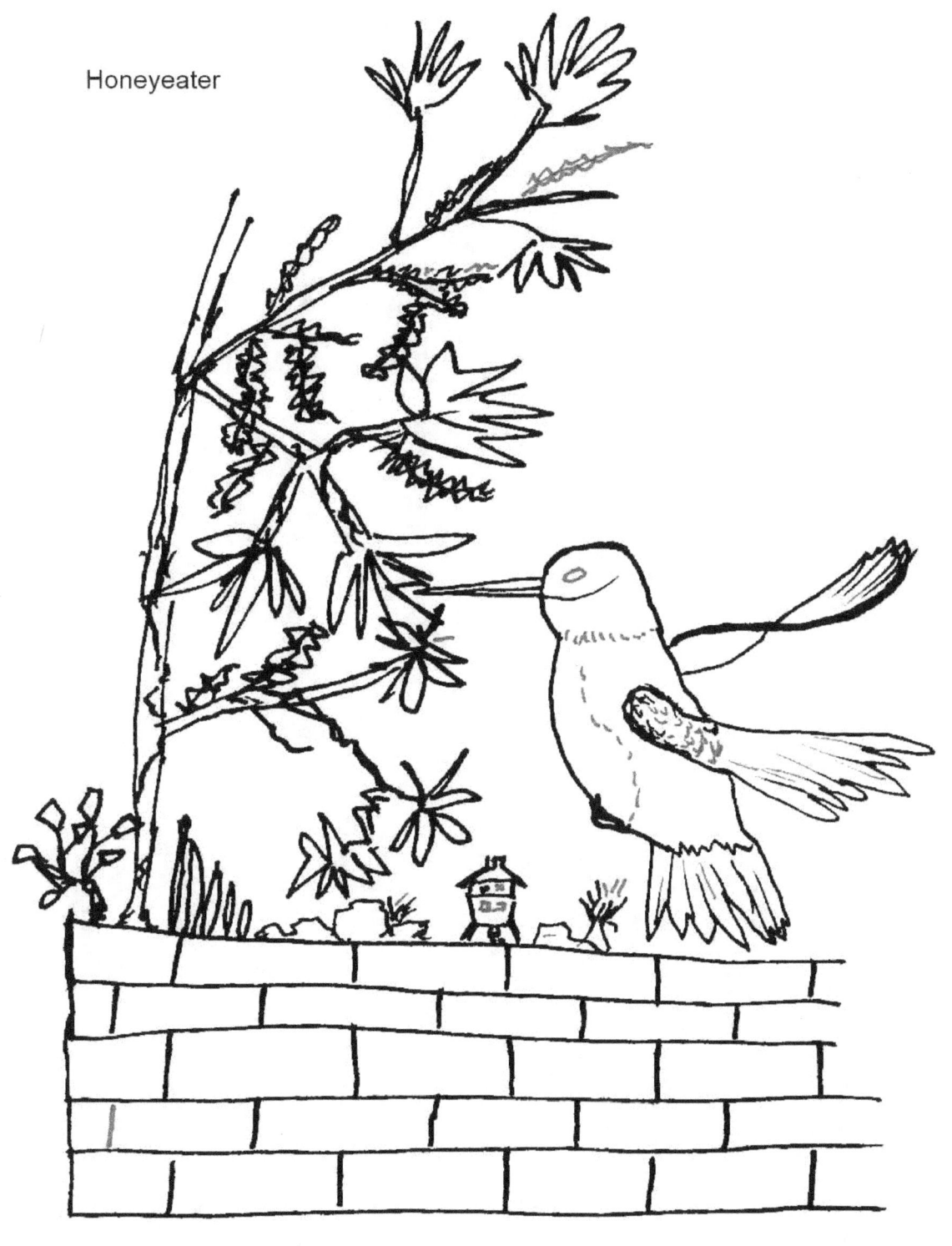

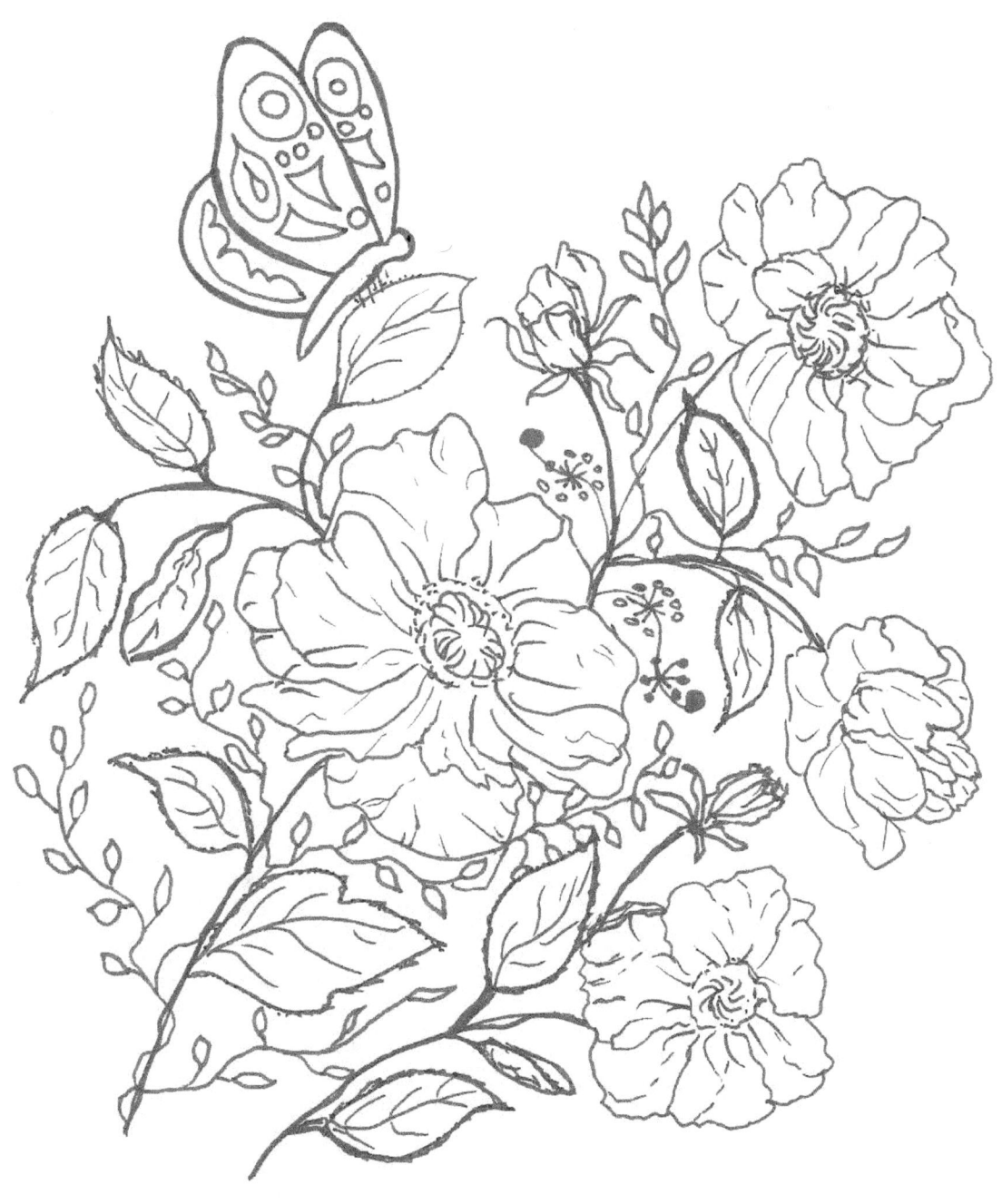

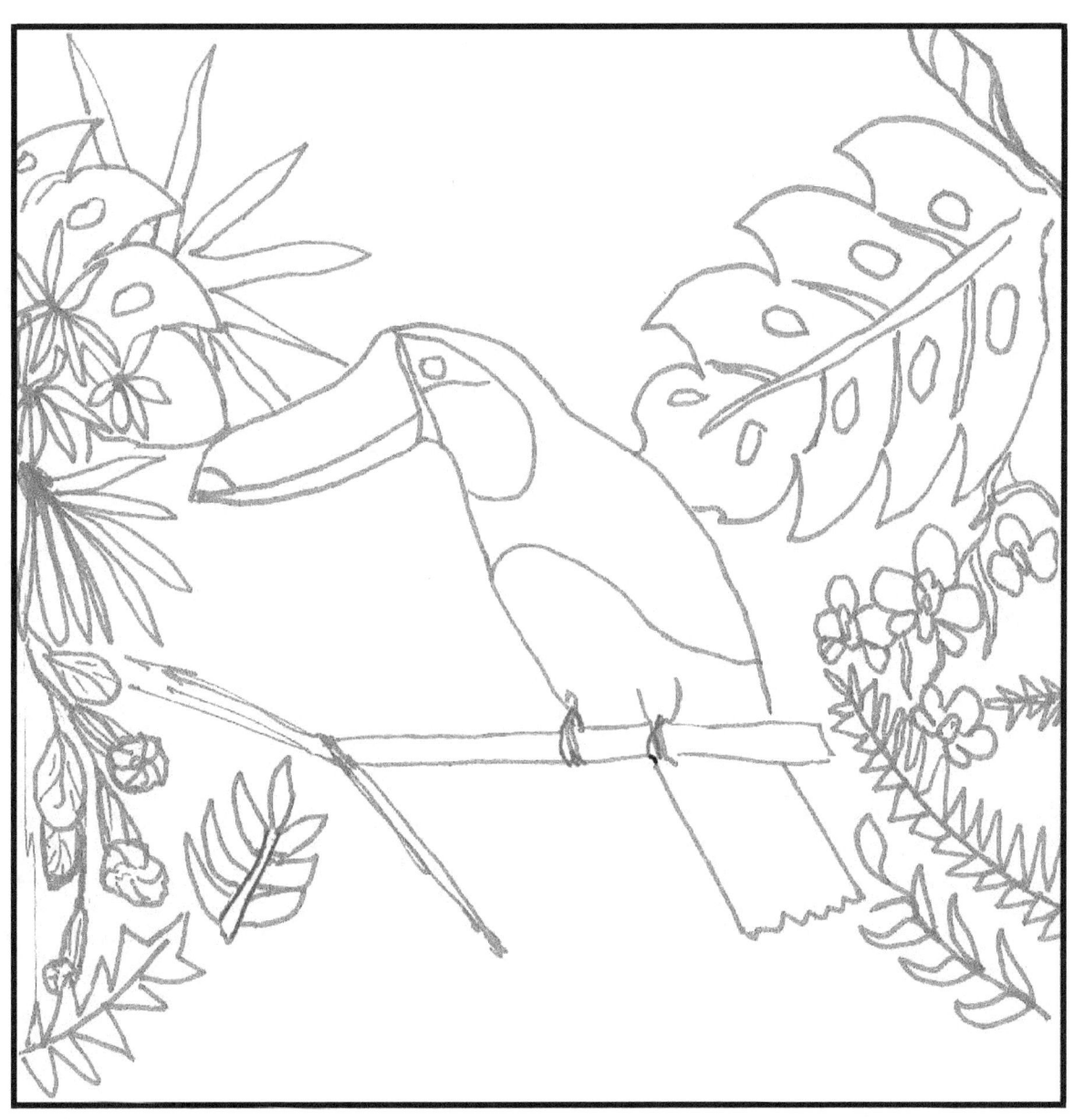

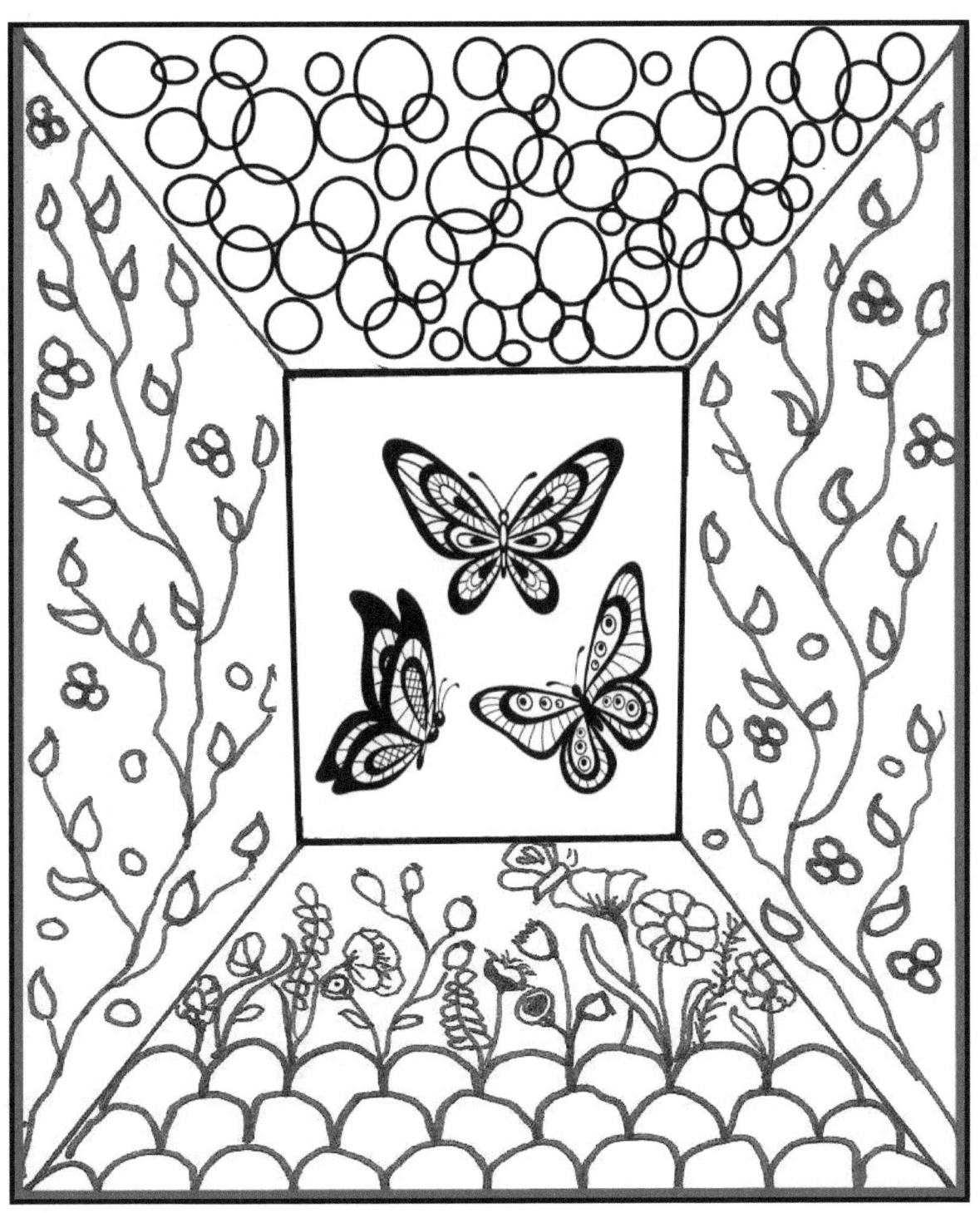

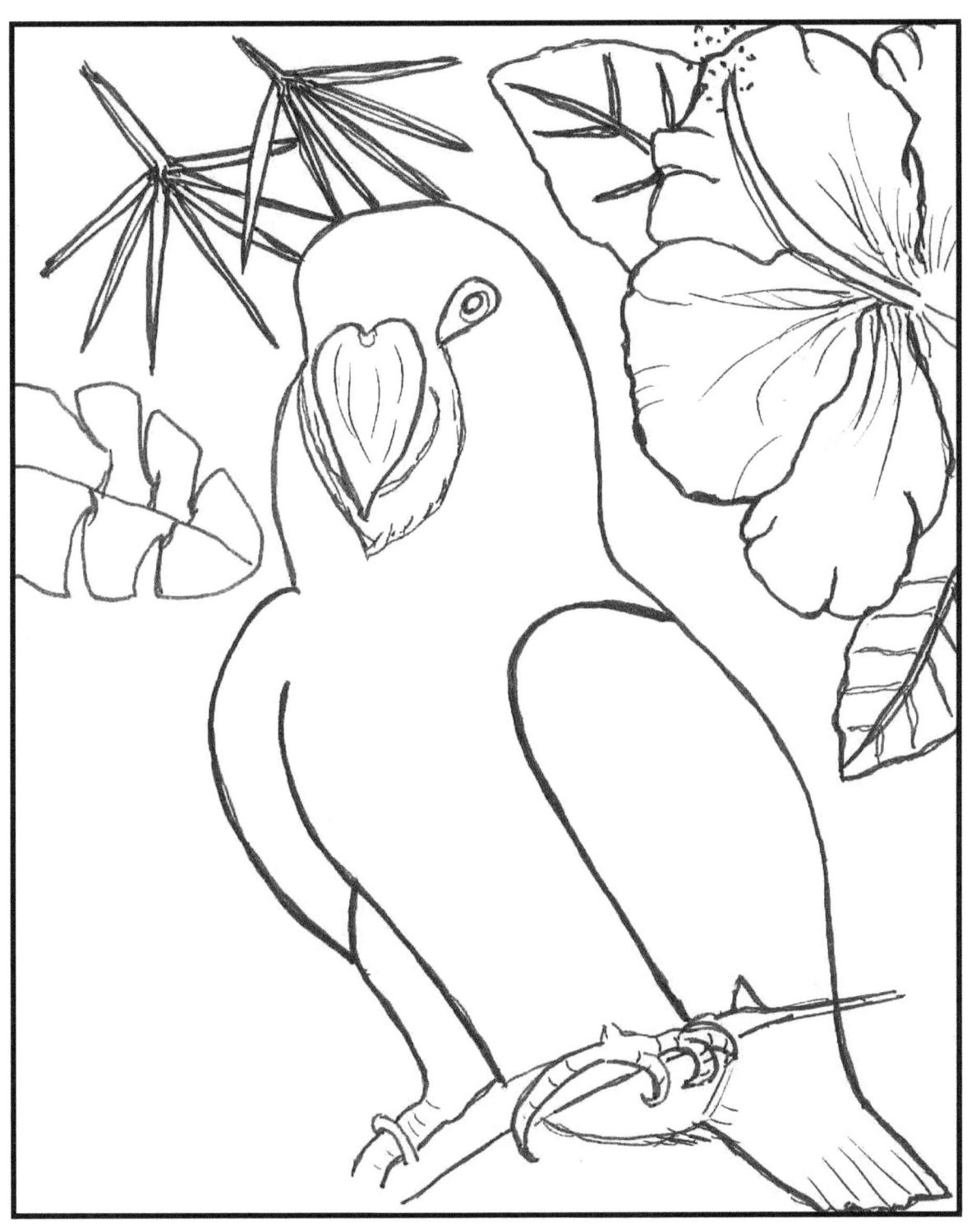

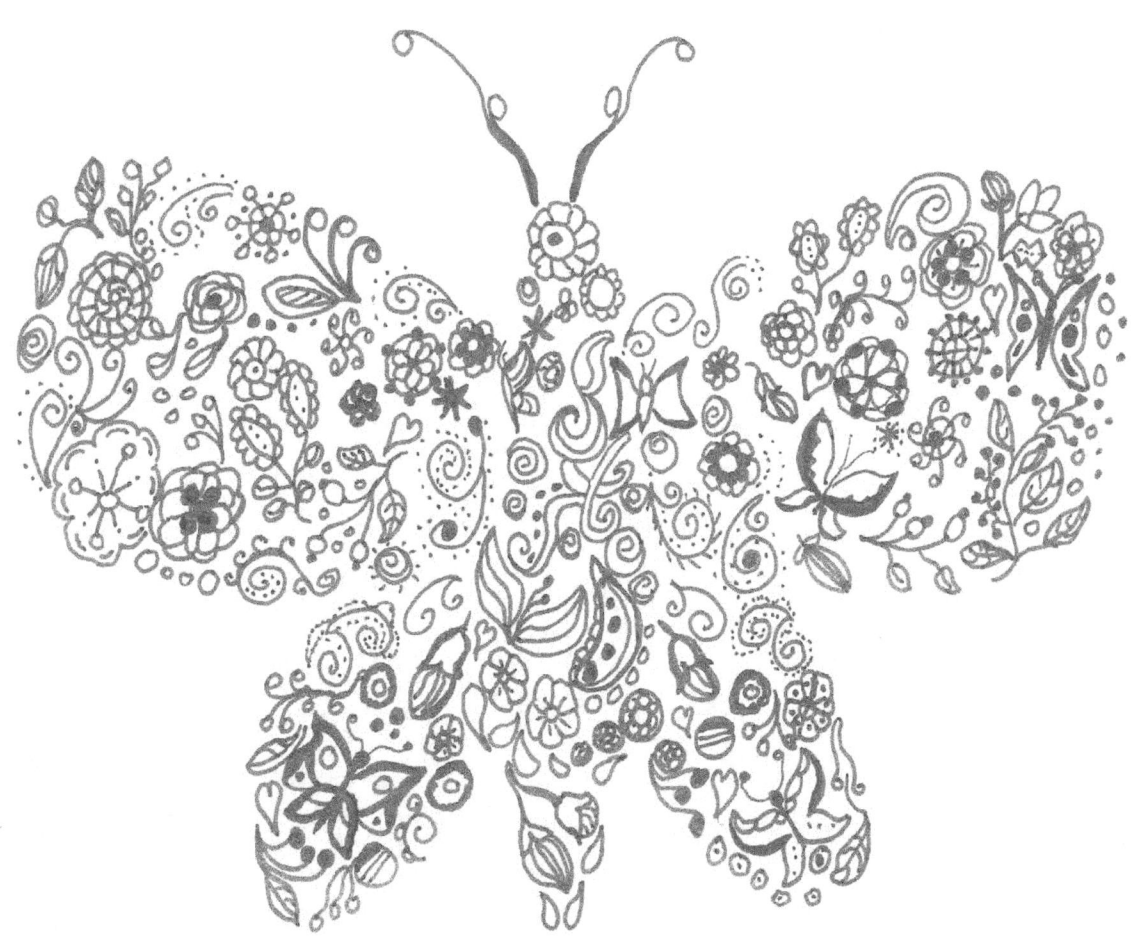

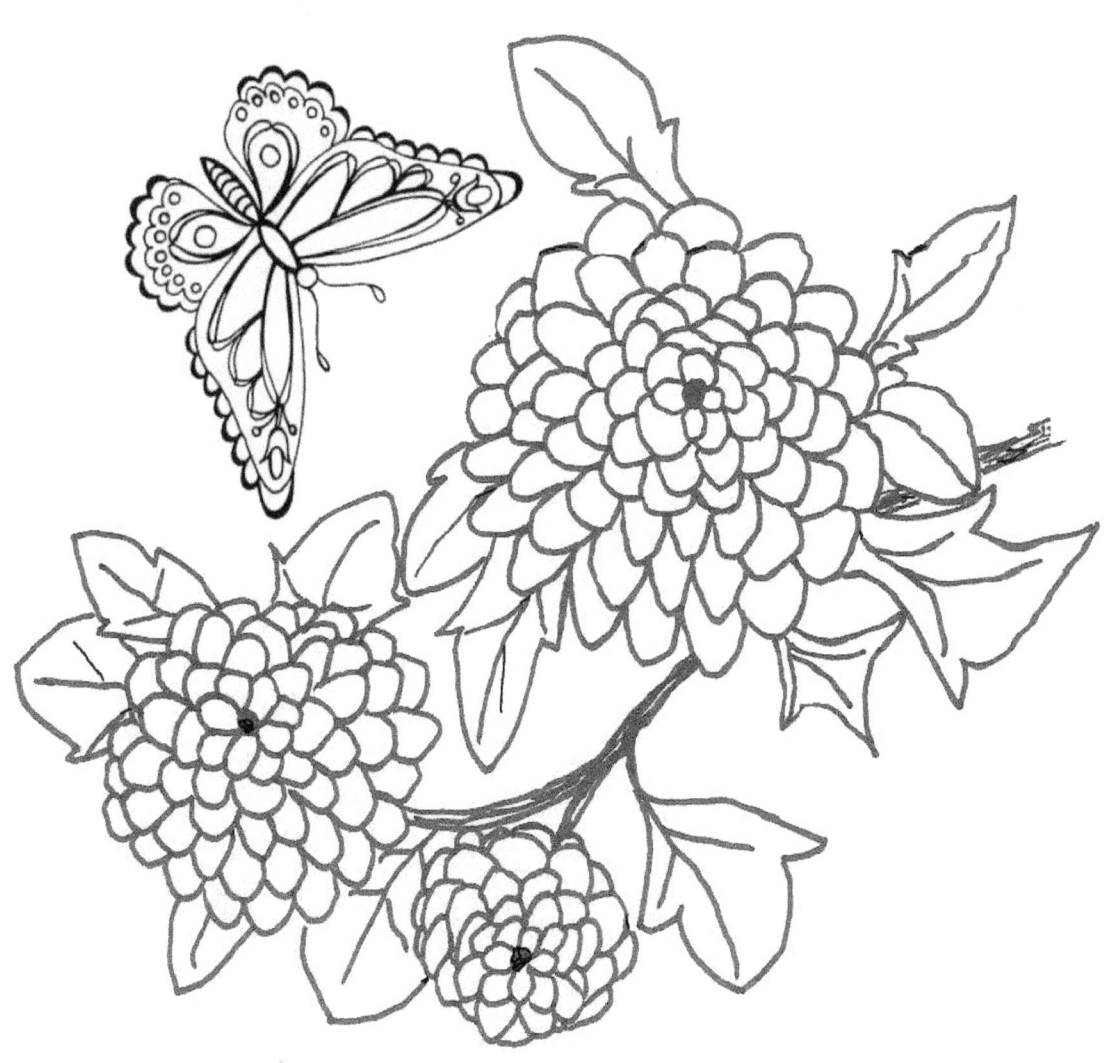

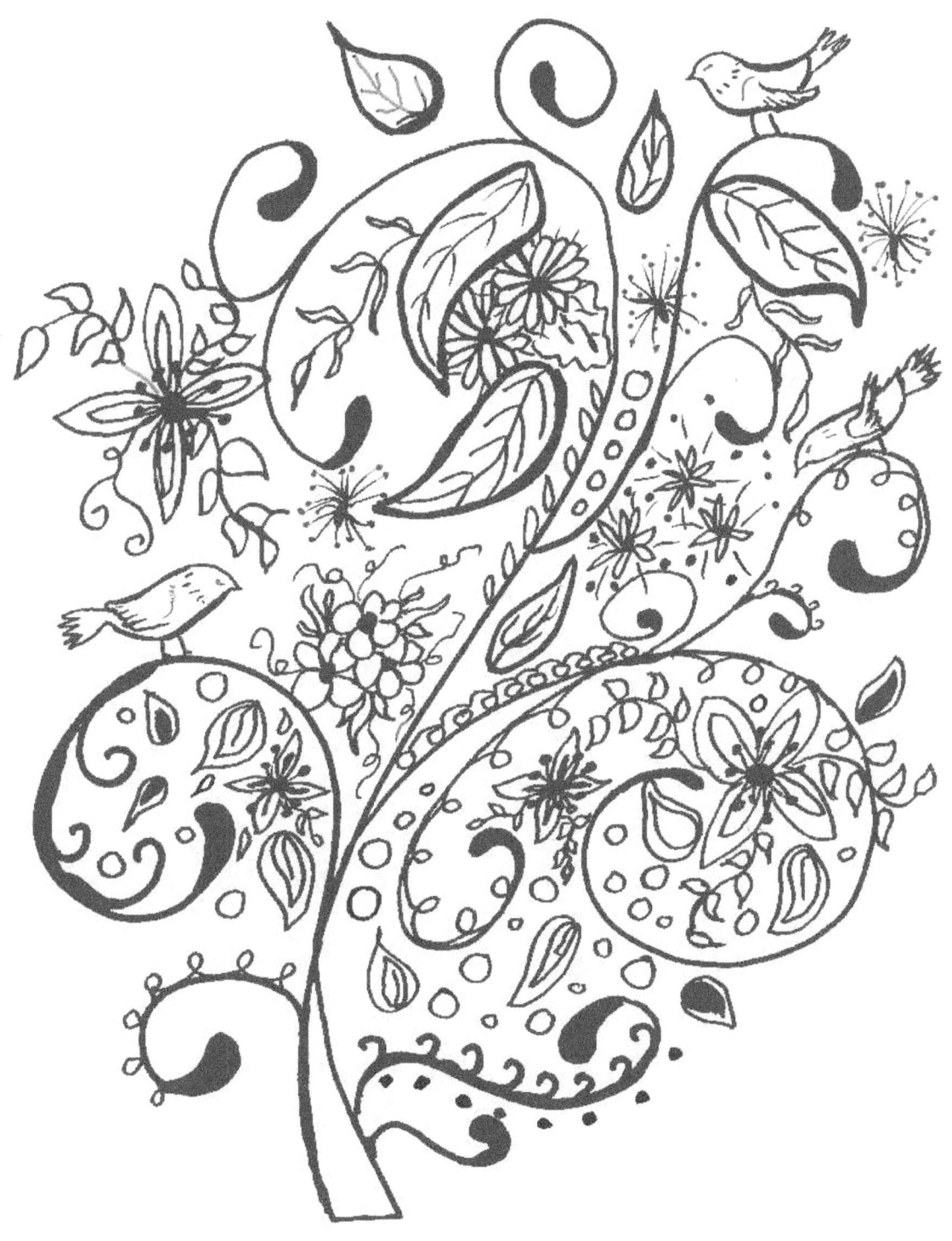

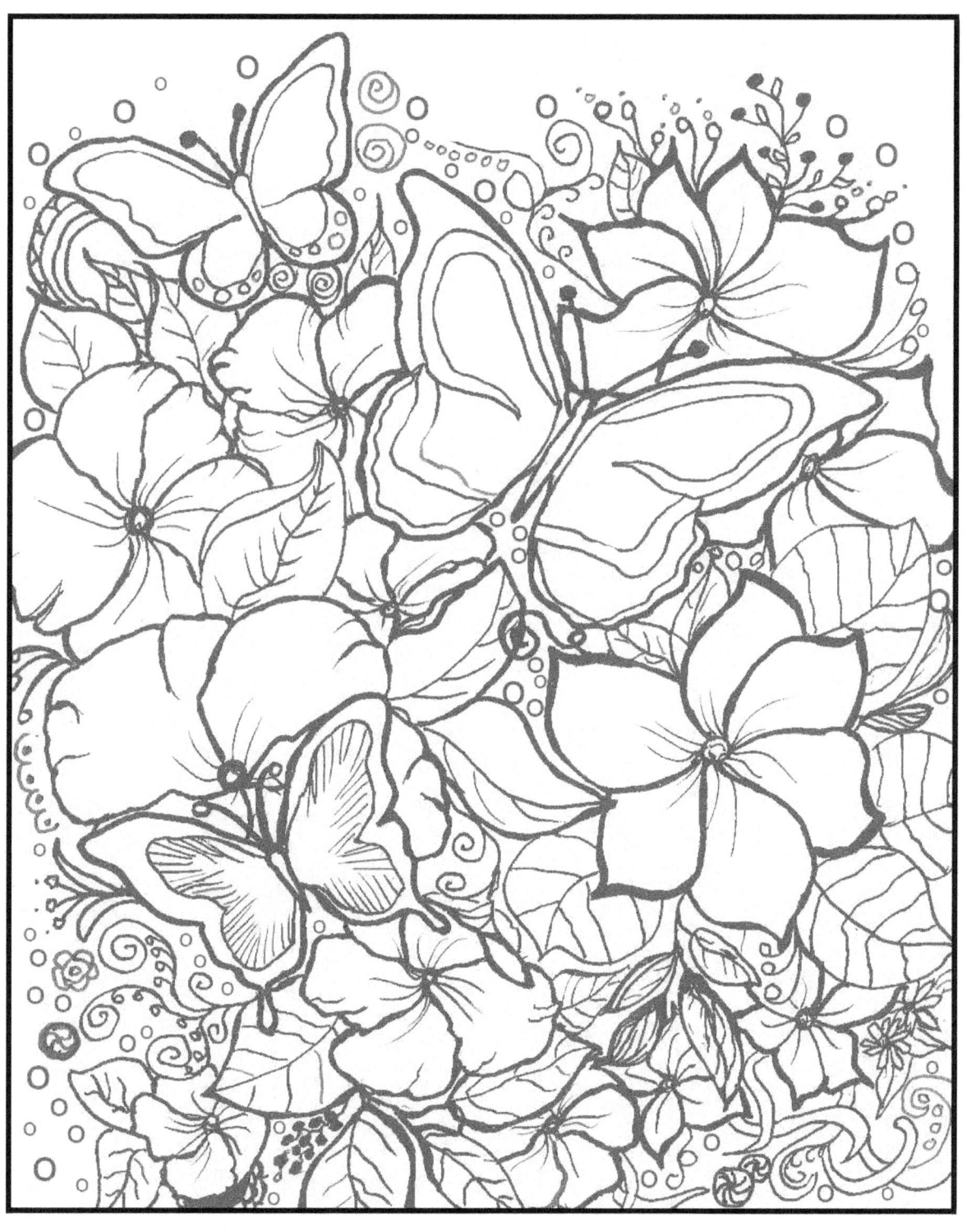

KD COLORING STUDIO

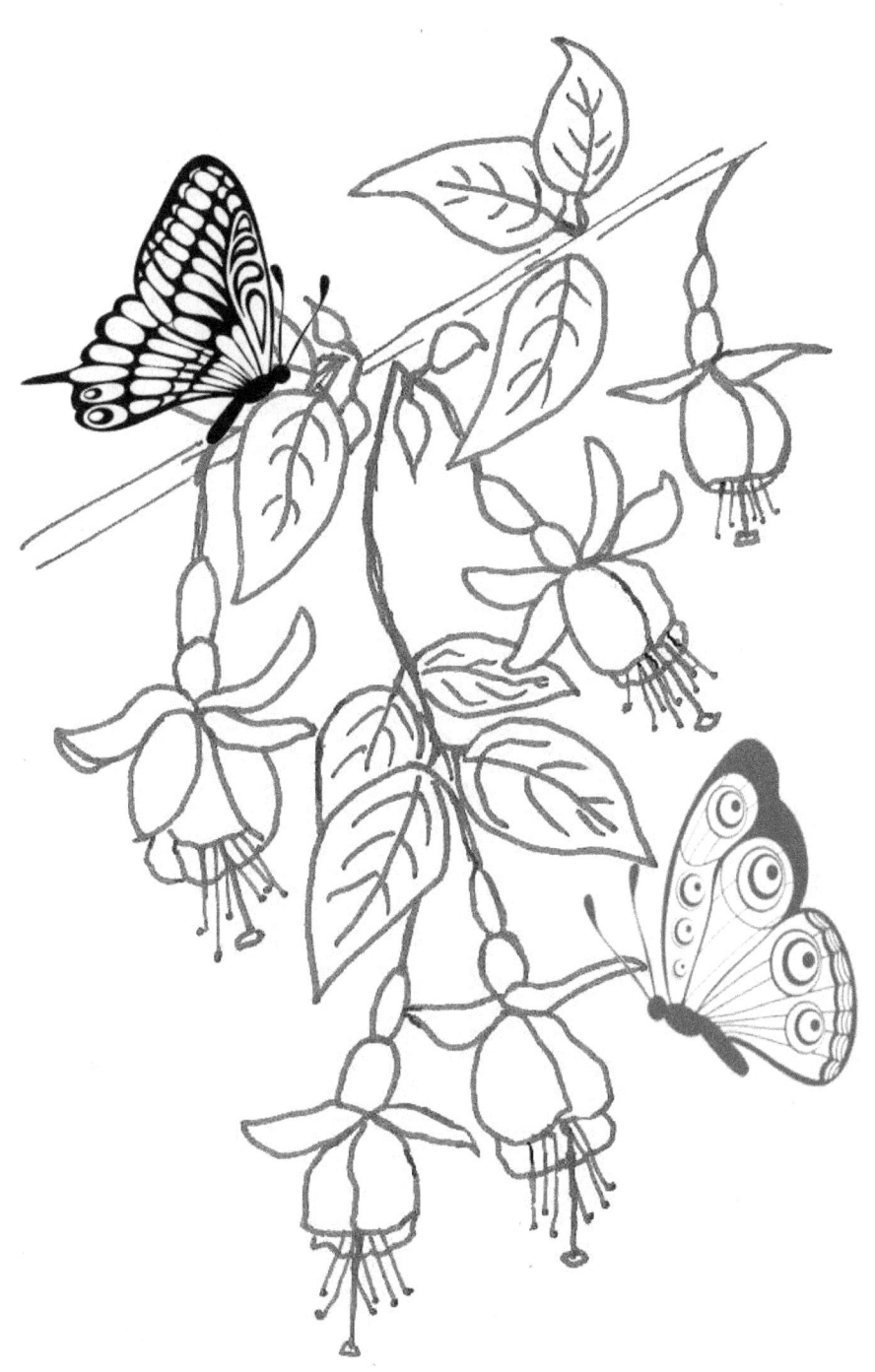

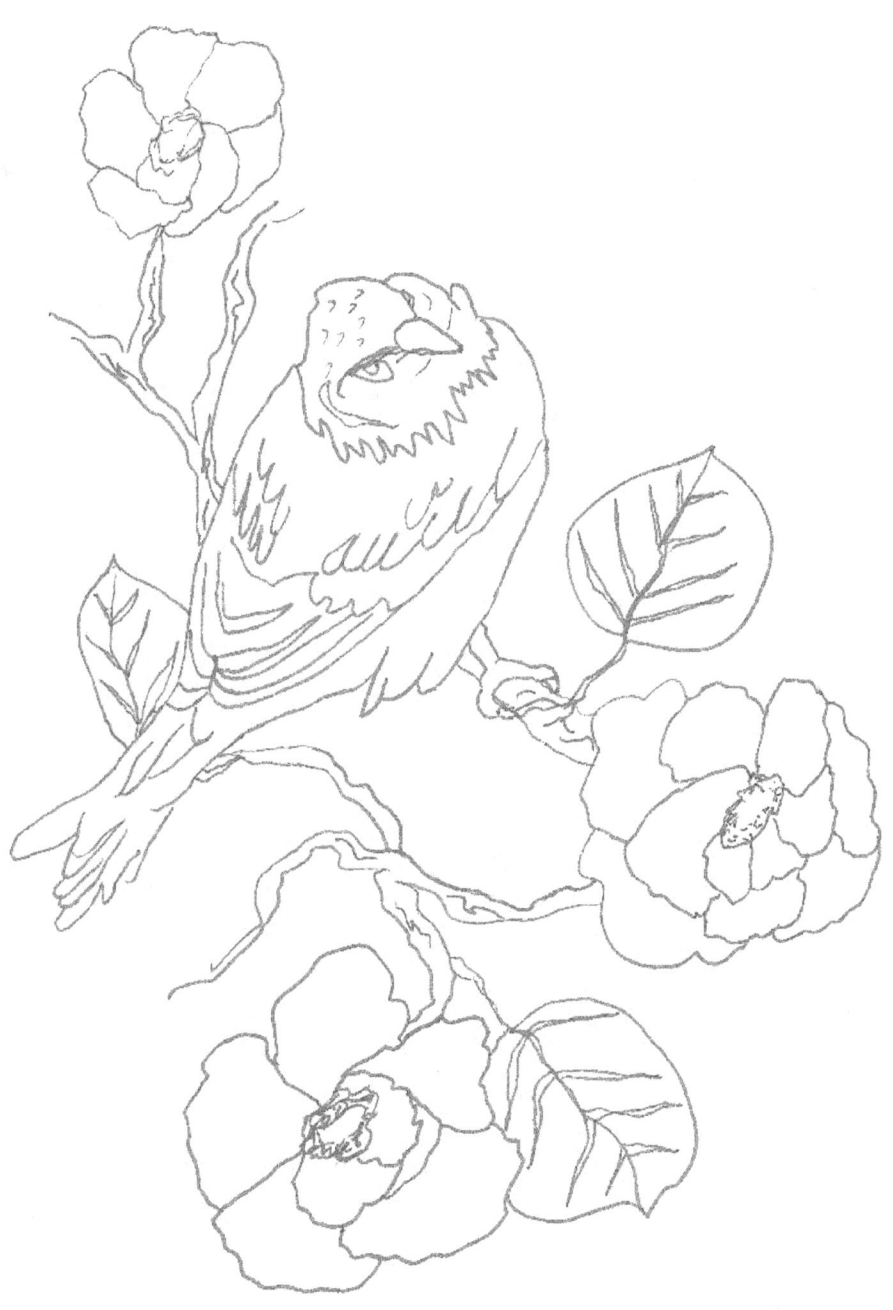

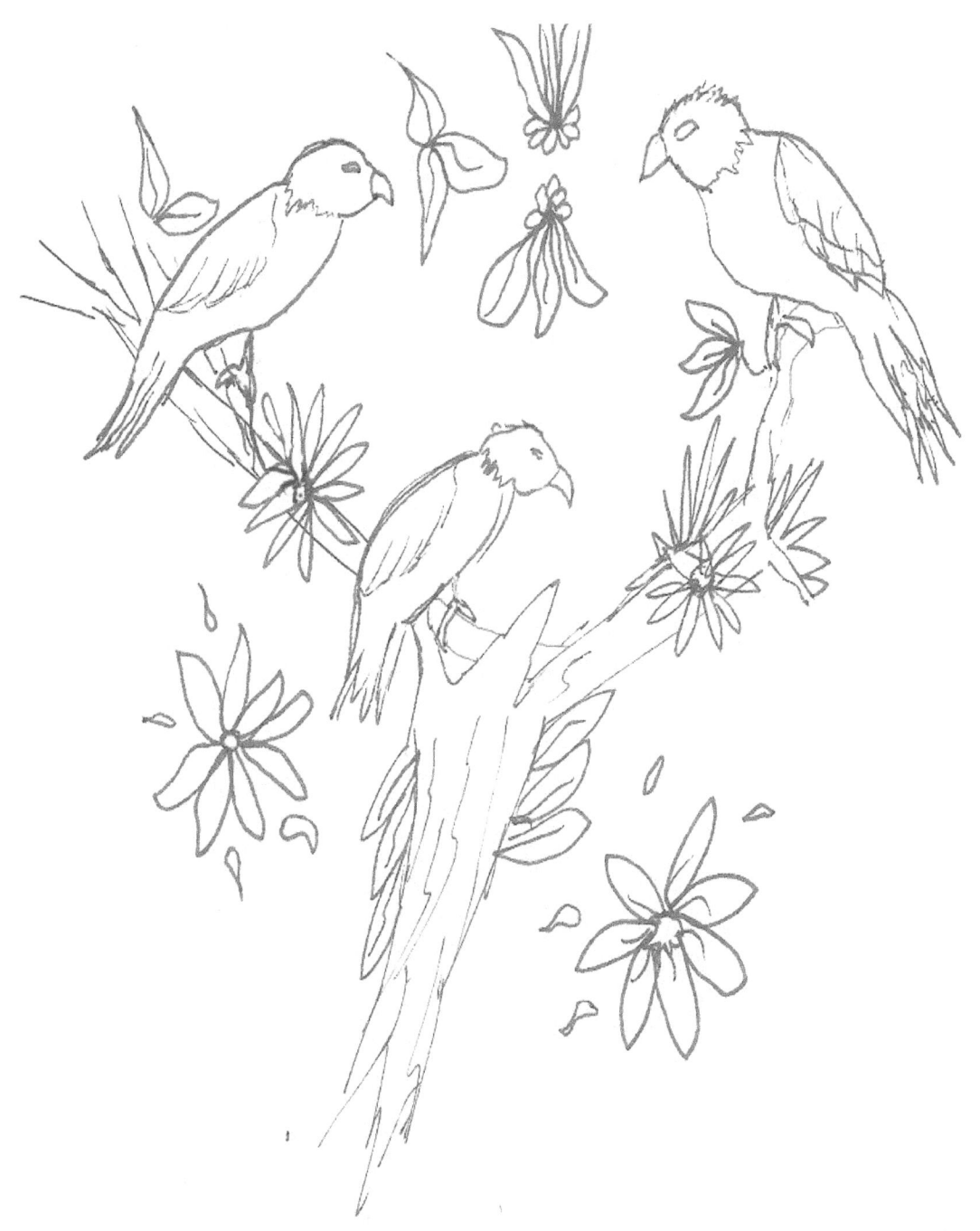

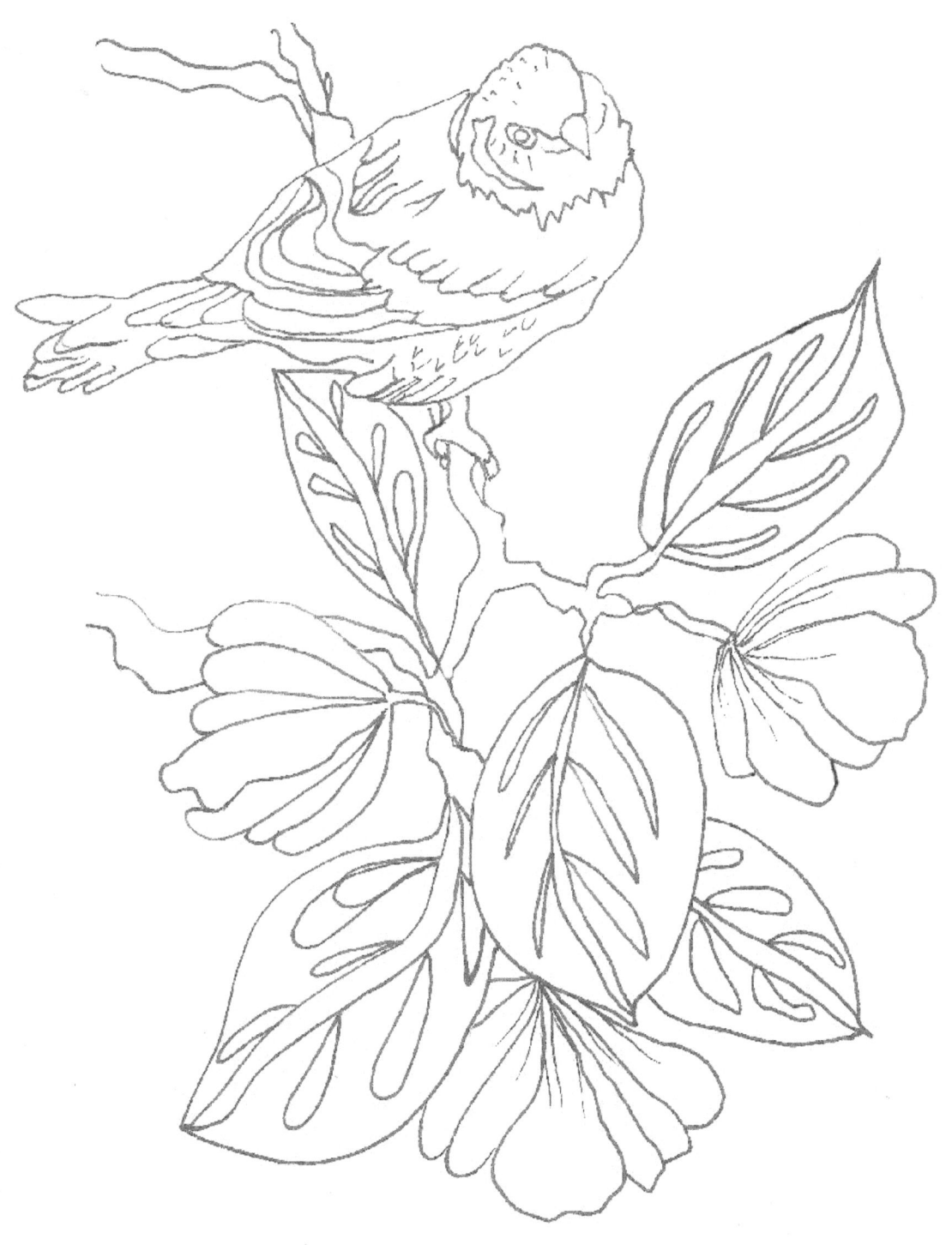

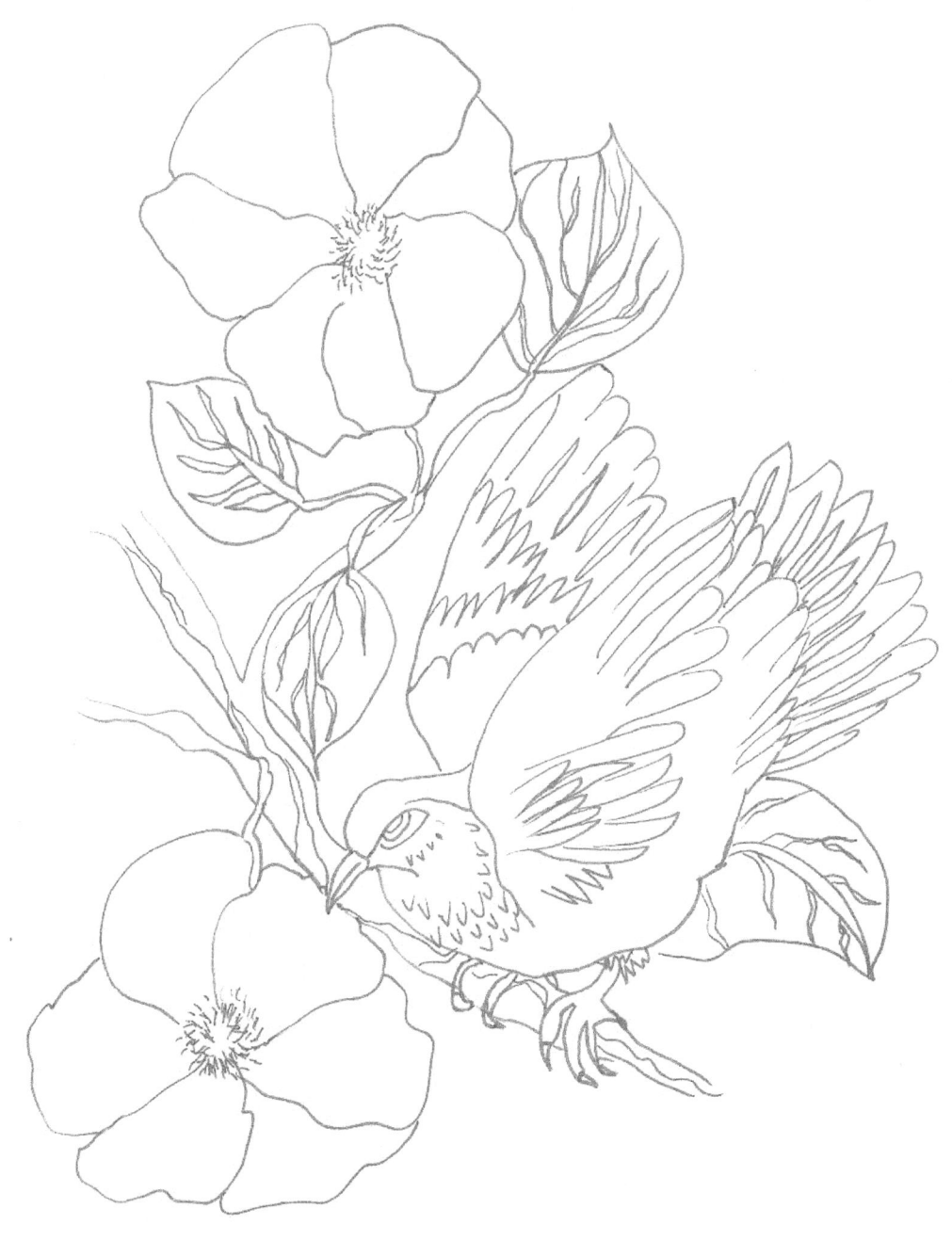

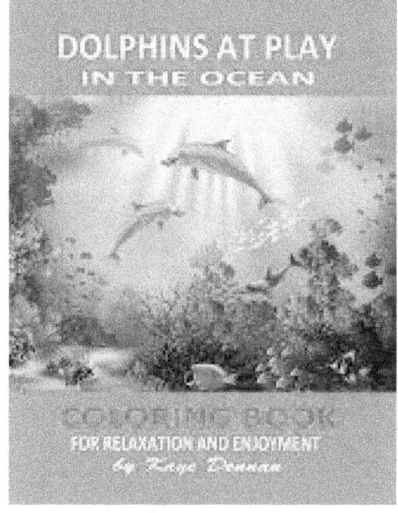
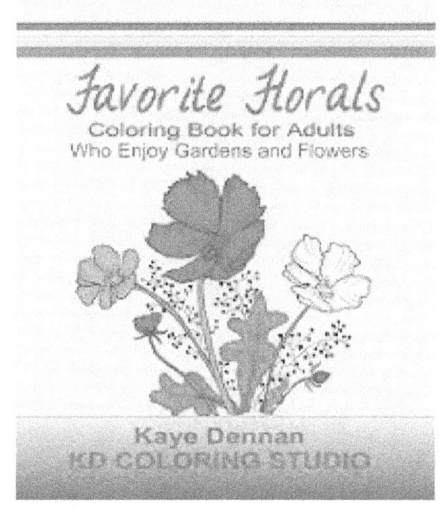
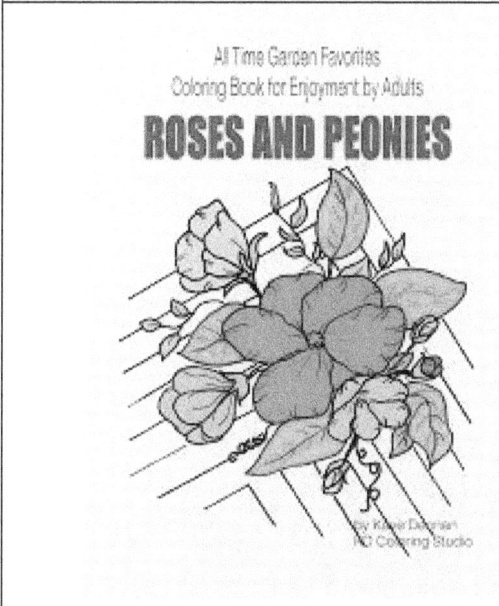
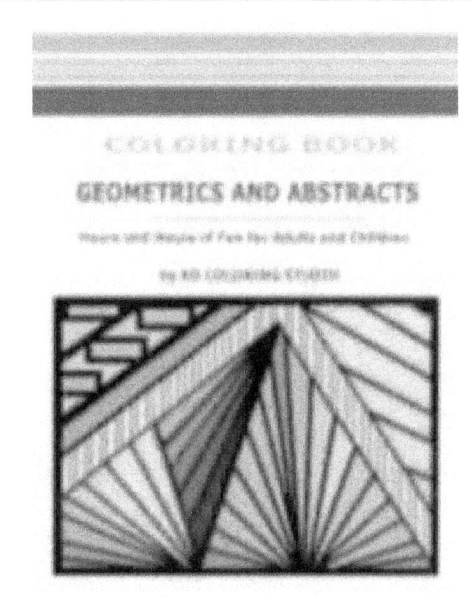

More paperback coloring books can be sourced through

KD COLORING STUDIO AT

http://kdcoloring.com

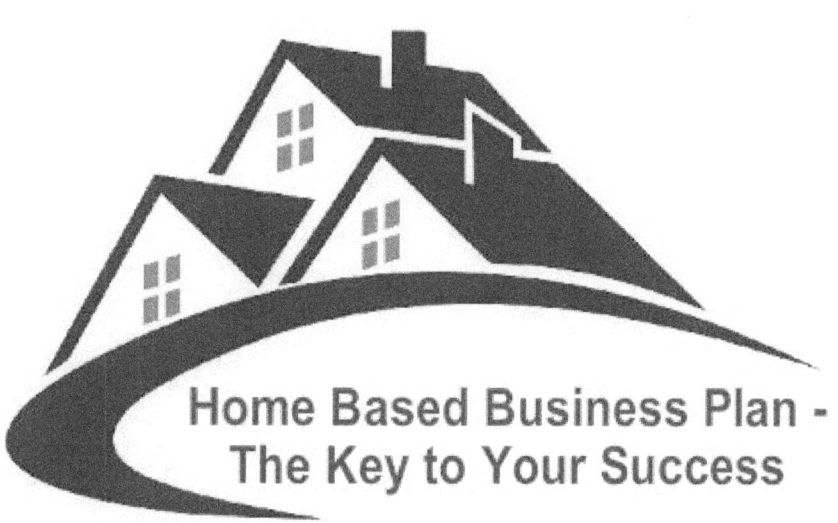